HINDUTVA

Jyotirmaya Sharma is professor of political science at the University of Hyderabad. His other recent publications include *Terrifying Vision: M.S. Golwalkar, the RSS and India* and *Cosmic Love and Human Apathy: Swami Vivekananda's Restatement of Religion*. He has also co-edited a volume with A. Raghuramaraju titled, *Grounding Morality: Freedom, Knowledge and the Plurality of Cultures* (2010). He has been fellow of the Swedish Collegium for Advanced Study, Lichtenberg-Kolleg – The Göttingen Institute of Advanced Study, Germany, Centre for the Study of Developing Societies and the Indian Institute of Advanced Study, Simla. The International House, Japan, awarded him the Asia Leadership Fellow Programme fellowship for 2008. Sharma also held senior editorial positions at *The Times of India* and *The Hindu* between 1998 and 2006, and continues to write columns for *Hindustan Times* and *Outlook*.

PRAISE FOR THE BOOK

'This is a clear and concise exploration of the writings of Dayanand Saraswati, Aurobindo, Vivekananda and Savarkar ...'

—Jawid Laiq, *Outlook*

'[Jyotirmaya Sharma] makes a valuable, well-considered contribution to the discussion on the anti-thesis of secularism.'

—*Frontline*

'An excavation of the intellectual genealogy of Hindutva is long overdue. What makes Sharma's book especially notable is that he is no Marxist secularist, but a Hindu steeped in his own cultural and religious tradition ... He also has a gift for communicating complex ideas in lucid prose.'

—*The Telegraph*

'Jyotirmaya Sharma's book, perhaps for the first time, presents a detailed descriptive and historical account of both the idea of Hindutva and its historical developments. It fills an enormous gap, thus facilitating a better understanding of the term Hindutva.'

—*Seminar*

'An excellent guide into the individual thought of ... the most important Hindu nationalist ideologues.'

—*Biblio*

HINDUTVA

EXPLORING THE IDEA OF HINDU NATIONALISM

JYOTIRMAYA SHARMA

HarperCollins *Publishers* India

First published in 2003 by Penguin Books India
This edition published in India in 2015 by
HarperCollins *Publishers* India

P-ISBN: 978-93-5177-397-9
E-ISBN: 978-93-5177-398-6

2 4 6 8 10 9 7 5 3 1

HarperCollins *Publishers*
A-75, Sector 57, Noida, Uttar Pradesh 201301, India
1 London Bridge Street, London, SE1 9GF, United Kingdom
Hazelton Lanes, 55 Avenue Road, Suite 2900, Toronto, Ontario M5R 3L2
and 1995 Markham Road, Scarborough, Ontario M1B 5M8, Canada
25 Ryde Road, Pymble, Sydney, NSW 2073, Australia
195 Broadway, New York, NY 10007, USA

Typeset in 11/14 Sabon LT Std
By Saanvi Graphics Noida

Printed and bound at
Thomson Press (India) Ltd

For my teachers

M.V. Prasad, Ganesh Devy, Noël K. O'Sullivan, Gopal Krishna, Mrinal Miri

And

For Siddharth Varadarajan and Omair Ahmed, friends who showed real courage

CONTENTS

INTRODUCTION

When the reviews for this book in its previous life[1] started coming in, they only served to confirm Jorge Luis Borges's words. Speaking about whether writers ought to be affected by praise or criticism, Borges felt that an author 'can be done or undone by his own writing, not by what other people say of him…'.[2] Reflecting on their criticisms, the only conclusion that could be drawn was that this writer had been undone, to an extent, by his own writing. Two clarifications follow this confession. Firstly, there is very little in the substantive chapters in the book that requires alteration or even a second look. The essays on Dayananda Saraswati, Swami Vivekananda, Sri Aurobindo and Vinayak Damodar Savarkar continue to serve well the overall intent and theme of the book. But, secondly, the introduction to the earlier volume lacked assertiveness and even a degree of clarity. Individual essays had chronicled the contradictions, paradoxes and ambiguities of the four thinkers chosen here sufficiently without providing a nail to hang them on to. The voice of the author, in this instance, was faint, often tentative; the onus on the reader to decipher and construct a cohesive argument from within the individual essays was far too great. This volume is an attempt to address this limitation by offering a new introduction and also an additional essay at the end of the volume.

A pattern seemed to emerge from reading the more informed and thoughtful reviews of the 2003 edition. These, in turn, could be delineated into two broad themes. The first was the exhortation to see the emergence and reassertion of Hindutva politics in the last two decades as a social movement that sought to address the long-suppressed anxieties of the Hindus. It called for a greater sensitivity to the historical context. References to the Babri Masjid-Ramajanmabhoomi movement, the felling of the Babri Mosque, the riots in the aftermath of the demolition of the mosque, and also to Godhra and the post-Godhra riots were made and their cumulative memory invoked and carefully marked. These historical events were seen as the inevitable unfolding of religious, right-wing politics, but also perceived as unravelling of the sinister logic of certain forms of nationalism. Implicit in these criticisms were a number of suggestions: that Hindu nationalism was a relatively modern phenomenon, and that it could be easily understood if one looked at the tension that a clash between tradition and modernity produces. Also, if only a clear distinction could be wrought between various shades of nationalism, Hindutva politics would automatically stand clarified. In other words, explanation was sought from within the book to explain recent history, and, if such an understanding was made available, Hindutva and its politics would be rendered more comprehensible. Inadvertently, perhaps, the book was also read as another addition to the debate on Indian secularism on the one hand, and an outpouring of liberal pieties on the other. Let us address this first set of concerns straightaway.

In a recent essay in the *New York Review of Books*,[3] the philosopher Thomas Nagel, writing about the late historian Tony Judt's reading of American Jews and their preoccupation with the memory of the Holocaust, feels that this obsession with the Holocaust is a terrible mistake. Following Judt, Nagel argues that while the Holocaust provides them reference, liturgy, example, moral instruction and historical proximity, their relentless engagement with it is based on an error. They have, he argues, confused a means of remembering with a reason to do so. Are we really Jews, he asks, for no better reason than Hitler sought to exterminate our grandparents? Taking cue from Nagel and Judt, I would suggest that contemporary debates around Hindutva are only a means of interrogating the historical and conceptual unfolding of Hindu identity and the genealogy of Hindu nationalism. This is especially so because in the Indian context, two major predictions made by social scientists stand severely tested. The first was the proposition that as modernization and industrialization advance, the hold of religion over the lives of men and women would decline. The universal claims of the secularization thesis today are being vigorously questioned or altered to explain the continued salience of religion in many parts of the world, nowhere more so than in India and Asia. The second was the belief, shared by Marxists and liberals alike, that the hold of nationalism would decline with the erosion of ethnic and cultural differences; increase in industrialization, where mobility, communication, and the steady decline in the hold local communities and associations have over people would dismantle national loyalties. Once again, despite industrialization and mobility of people across the world, nationalism and its durability straddles countries and continents, much more so in India.

One of the clearest manifestations of a spurt in religiosity and the reassertion of national sentiment is to be found in the resurgence of Hindu nationalism in India. Its growing strength in the past two decades has led to violence between Hindus and Muslims, between Hindus and Christians, and its votaries have periodically questioned India's democratic, republican, rational and secular foundations. The rise of religious nationalism of this kind also brings into sharp focus the larger question of the ability of liberalism and democracy to withstand the onslaught of an emotive call to 'culture' and 'traditional values'. Sometimes powerful images of violence, including riots, growing instances of intolerance, questioning and emasculating the liberal space and regression into an imagined glorious past are seen as all that Hindutva represents. This is far from true. This is merely a fraction of the ideological and political ambition of Hindutva; a regular and organised unfolding of 'everyday Hindutva'. But there is more to Hindutva than just episodic outbursts of rhetoric and action.

Hindu nationalists have argued that definitions of nationalism and identity in India are inextricably linked with the recognition of Hinduism as the defining and deciding factor. They argue that the nation is nothing but the physical and emotional outcome of Hindu aspirations. The question of identity for them, therefore, is an issue that is naturally settled in favour of a clearly delineated Hindu identity, while Muslims and Christians are 'outsiders' and could be part of India only after they accept the 'national culture'. Despite these claims, the question of Hindu identity remains unresolved, equally among Hindu nationalists as well as scholars seeking to find answers to this vexed question. In recent years, scholars like David N. Lorenzen[4] have asked the question, 'who invented Hinduism?' and have given answers that echo the methodology, if not the politics of the Hindu nationalists, namely, that Hinduism was invented as a consequence of the encounter between Islam and the Hindus. Identity is, then, reducible to a staged encounter between the 'Self' and its threatening 'Other'.

Efforts to clarify issues relating to Hindu identity have been limited to either extending the insights of Edward Said in his monument work, *Orientalism*, or one that is in the form of Wendy Doniger's magisterial *The Hindus: An Alternative History*, a work that provokes and intervenes, almost surreptitiously, in the current debates on Hindu nationalist assertion. To others, the 'imagined communities' argument seems compelling, but leaves an important question unanswered: why is it that the fabrication of imagined communities, triggered by modern nationalism, leads to the quest for a rational and scientific past, rejecting the claims of myths and the expressive force of narrative sources? Even those who are seeking to create an imaginary past, then, remain beholden to the lure of what constitutes a 'fact', looking to authenticate that imaginary past in epigraphic, numismatic and archaeological data. While these forms of evidence are invaluable, the question of identity can hardly be resolved through purely scientific history. The way forward, however, requires a new approach and a different treatment to the question of Hindu identity.

In recent years, the works of Sumit Sarkar, Francesca Orsini, Ganesh Devy, Sheldon Pollock, Tanika Sarkar,

Heinrich Von Stietencron, Raymond Schwab, Partha Chatterjee, Vasudha Dalmia, Richard Eaton, John Zavos, T.N. Madan, Christophe Jeffrelot, Dipankar Gupta, Paul Brass, Thomas Blom Hansen, Herman Kulke, Peggy Froerer, Günther-Dietz Sontheimer, Ashis Nandy, Andrew J. Nicholson and Romila Thapar, to name only a few, have greatly taken forward the task of clarifying important dimensions emerging out of the issues surrounding Hindu identity. Despite these insights, an enterprise of this nature requires a different register, a deliberate and purposeful harmony between the philosophical, literary, historical and sociological modes. The work that comes close to what is being proposed here is the Japanese sociologist Eiji Oguma's *A Genealogy of 'Japanese' Self-Images.*[5] Oguma's book is a remarkable effort in historical sociology, but tends to lean excessively on the side of Weberian sociology and factors in a rather sweeping historical canvas. It begins by addressing political questions relating to the rise of right-wing nationalism in Japan, but considers them ultimately irrelevant; the idea that the moment the mirror of Japanese self-images is broken, the political questions will automatically resolve themselves.

This brings us to the second set of criticisms. All commentators made a distinction between Hindutva and Hinduism, perceiving the latter to be more plural, tolerant, eclectic and 'pure'. Hindutva was seen as a deviant, distorted and perverted manifestation of Hinduism. They felt that conflating Vivekananda and Aurobindo with the likes of Savarkar was an error: for them Vivekananda and Aurobindo had non-Hindutva elements in them. They charged that allowing Vivekananda and Aurobindo to keep Savarkar's company was a way of facilitating their appropriation by the Hindu nationalists. Here were two assumptions at play, that the sheer plurality of Hinduism would axiomatically produce tolerance, understanding and non-violence, and, secondly, that thinkers like Vivekananda and Aurobindo contained within themselves both emancipatory and regressive elements; the mere fact of disengaging them with someone like Savarkar would somehow enhance their redeeming side. Put differently, the framework within which notions of 'tradition', 'culture' and 'national culture' developed and 'sought legitimation can be located in the various seemingly authoritative restatements of Hinduism in the nineteenth century. They continue to exist as indicators of religion and religious identity but also can easily slide into representing secularized notions of nationalism, patriotism, national character and state ideology. Here is a list of a few of these:

- The non-violent Hindu;
- The tolerant Hindu;
- The mild Hindu;
- The inward-looking and spiritually inclined Hindu;
- The non-materialistic Hindu;
- The non-converting, non-proselytizing Hindu;
- Hindus never attack until provoked in the extreme;
- Hindus have always given the world spiritual wisdom.

In other words, the nineteenth-century restatements of Hinduism provide a set of shared myths, acceptable to secularists and fundamentalists, to left-liberals and free-market apologists, alike. This is the point where the distinction between Hindutva and Hinduism, perceiving the latter to be more plural, tolerant, eclectic and 'pure' and Hindutva as the deviant, distorted and perverted manifestation of Hinduism, collapses.

This volume makes no such claims of an imagined distinction. Even in the earlier introduction, the reason for the inclusion of Dayananda, Vivekananda and Aurobindo was explicitly stated:

> A first step towards challenging Hindutva through the means of a conversation is to be more open-minded about the possibility of such a conversation. To achieve this, the next logical step is to be more sceptical about our own tradition, question self-assumed identities and question the voice and authority of traditionally privileged individuals, icons and texts. Indeed, this constitutes the explicit theme of this book. It looks at certain distinctive restatements of Hinduism and Hindu identity in the nineteenth and twentieth centuries. It is an attempt to understand four influential answers to two central questions: Who is a Hindu? What is Hinduism? Maharshi Dayananda Saraswati, Swami Vivekananda, Sri Aurobindo and V.D. Savarkar provided answers to these questions in ways that remain significant to this day. Savarkar's concept of Hindutva can be seen as the most mature and the most extreme manifestation of this quest for a definitive Hindu identity.

In other words, this book does not make any distinction between Hinduism and Hindutva. What it explicitly argues is that Hindutva is the dominant expression of Hinduism in our times. By no means does the argument suggest that it is the only way in which Hinduism expresses itself today, but, to use a musical metaphor, Hindutva is the note on which the stress falls.

This book, therefore, is the first step in arriving at a longer and deeper genealogy of Hindu identity and its contemporary manifestation in the form of Hindutva. In taking these preliminary, yet sure, steps, the attempt was to raise questions and insert markers that would begin to prepare the ground for situating the longer and deeper genealogy that Hindu identity merits. In this sense, the essays presented here move away from the impulse to propose a museumized 'archaeology' of Hindutva to building a genealogy.[6] In doing so, I propose five steps as a way of fabricating this genealogy, moving away from what a fixation with Hindutva politics of the day allows. While the essays in this volume do not identify these steps neatly and rigidly, each of these resonates through the book and the overall narrative faithfully reflects their salience. These are:

1. To delineate the foundation myths of the Hindus. Since the very idea of the 'Hindu' as a universal category is a recent one, the search for foundation myths will reveal the politics of these myths. The sheer multiplicity of rendering of a myth over time and space will also afford a glimpse into questions of memory, time and a plurality of histories. It is no accident that Coomaraswamy translated myth as itihāsa (history), and suggested that it was 'the penultimate truth, of which all experience is the temporal reflection'.
2. To arrive at a methodology of reading the puranic literature, so that an entire textual tradition that is

rich in myths and legends can be better understood. Even today, the puranas are read from the perspective of the dominant classical tradition and rejected as containing little truth. At best, they are seen as an attempt by the brahminical orthodoxy to absorb heterodox elements and mould them within the dominant tradition. The process by which this is done and its politics would be instructive in understanding the ways in which Hindu identity formation from the nineteenth century onwards rejected the puranas as a litany of falsehoods, only to be rejected in favour of a return to the Vedas and the Vedantic tradition represented by the Upanishads.

3. To map the ways in which the early Brahminic religion and the new sects that eventually arose from it coped with the doctrinal challenges of Jainism and Buddhism. This will clarify two issues. In the absence of any universalizing notion of Hinduism during the time of Mahavira and the Buddha, the ways in which various schools of philosophy, different sects and ordinary people coped with the challenges thrown by Jainism and Buddhism would be instructive in knowing how contemporary Hinduism's past dealt with an 'Other' that was not necessarily foreign and antagonistic, but came from within the doctrinal interstices of its own texts, rituals and practices. When thinkers like Dayananda, Vivekananda, Aurobindo and Savarkar uniformly denounced the Buddha and Buddhism for the decline of Hinduism and its fighting impulses, leading to India's enslavement in the hands of foreigners, is this attitude towards Buddhism original to the nineteenth century or has earlier antecedents? Secondly, it will

put in perspective arguments that a Hindu identity worth its name came into existence only with the coming of Islam.

4. The questions that have been asked as part of the question of Hindu identity since the nineteenth century inevitably are broken down into two questions: a) who is a Hindu? b) What is Hinduism? There is a flawed, yet alluring, conflation here of an empirical question with one that is normative. In every single instance since the nineteenth century, one or the other of these above questions is asked and the answer leads to the other. Set in another context, the same set of questions are never asked about the ancient civilizations of Greece, Rome, Egypt and China. This conflation has also led to banalities like 'Hinduism is a way of life'. Consigning Hinduism as a way of life shies away from the question that becomes imperative, and is, indeed, a political question: whose way of life? Therefore, it is suggested that an entirely different question ought to be posed that saves a study of Hindu identity from obvious category mistakes: what does a Hindu do? If this can be answered, the next question, 'what do Hindus do?', will bring the focus back to questions of history, politics, power and violence rather than essentializing Hindus or Hinduism as an inward-looking, mild, non-threatening and other-worldly people, who are only so because their religion happens to be Hinduism.
5. Finally to map the distance between Hindu identity as understood in all its forms in the last two centuries and the distance between its past and present. This has often been explained away as a story of the

> colonization, modernity, and the semitization of Hinduism. In other instances, contemporary Hindu identity has been dismissed as a perversion or a deviation of something that was pure, unalloyed and glorious. But if there is a chasm that lies between the past and the present, it needs to be explained in terms of the politics of the accretion of Hindu identity rather than in quasi-romantic notions of a golden age or the biblical idea of the Fall.

This is the foundation upon which this book is built. It is by no stretch of imagination a project that is complete or was intended to be definitive about the ideas that it ventured to explore. Rather, it was a first reconnaissance of the ideas that would eventually find greater clarity in subsequent works.

A word needs to be said about the essays in this volume. The first edition in 2003 had suggested that there were common elements that linked these individual thinkers. Some readers and critics have sought to disentangle these links by categorizing Vivekananda and Aurobindo as more spiritually inclined while likening Savarkar as an outright nationalist. Others sought to see Vivekananda, Dayananda and Aurobindo as reformists and Savarkar as a revivalist. Many of these concerns have been addressed above.

If there is a dissonance that separates Dayananda, Vivekananda and Aurobindo from Savarkar it is the language, tone and method of articulation. Dayananda was direct, acerbic, contentious, and, in places, even abusive. In sharp contrast, Vivekananda was rhetorical, eloquent, energetic, emotional, long-winded and driven.

Aurobindo was always the quintessential philosopher – grand, dry and systematic. Savarkar was a bit of all these. He was eloquent, direct, splenetic, dry, systematic and grand. The only thing he was lacking in was emotion. Binding them all together was a singular vision of Hindu India and its destiny. In fabricating this ideal, they were equally radical, extreme and militant. There is still merit, therefore, in rehearsing those features that reflect the striking similarity in the ideas of the thinkers included here. Neither are these common features among them accidental nor are they merely hostage to historical context: they are part of the history of ideas that the search for a Hindu identity constituted.

This terrible and tortured vision of the four shared a few characteristics. The first, and the most important, feature of this enterprise was to transform Hinduism into a rigid, codified, monochromatic entity. There was little scope for diversity of opinion, practices, rituals, observances and individual choices. Myths and legends were frowned upon. Local colour and flavour was seen as deviations from a grand ideal. To admit to infinite variations within the faith was seen as a sign of weakness. The Hindu nation had to be founded on racial and doctrinal unity. Hindus had to be bound together with the help of one book, one 'church' and one 'gospel'. This exercise itself took curious forms. In Dayananda, it amounted to the *exclusion* of everyone who did not adhere to Dayananda's interpretation of the Vedas. On the other hand, Savarkar sought to *include* the Sikhs, Jains and the Buddhists in his quest to define who is a Hindu.

The idea of Hinduism as a masculine, aggressive and violent faith is the second feature of this vision. India's slavery had to be explained; this was done in terms of loss of masculinity of the Hindus. The Buddha, the Jains, certain strands of Hindu metaphysics and theories of non-violence and non-harm were identified as the culprits that made Hindus effeminate. Hindus had to learn to live and die for an ideal. They had to fight wars, if need be, kill, destroy and plunder in order to preserve the core of national life. This core was religion. If they did not do so, they were likely to be swallowed by either alien faiths or by forces more powerful than them. The Islamic invasion and the British power in India did not come merely as another set of proselytizing sects; they came with gunpowder and the power of technology. It was not important for an individual or a nation to examine the truth or falsity of a proposition. Philosophically, non-violence might be a very noble idea. But blind adherence to it could wipe out the very traces of one's cultural exclusivity and identity. Every nation, therefore, demanded a certain degree of blind fidelity to certain goals and it was a sign of manliness to pursue these, even at the cost of one's life, if necessary. Action, therefore, was more important than the loftiest metaphysics.

Every faith must, inevitably, define its relationship with other faiths. Dayananda, Vivekananda, Aurobindo and Savarkar reduced this encounter of Hinduism into a story of confrontation and misfortune. This is the third characteristic of the Hindutva vision. The premise that Hinduism was the most ancient, the most perfect and the most evolved of all existing faiths was basic. It was seen, in fact, as the mother of all religions. Hinduism had nothing to learn from other faiths; indeed, it had a great deal to teach them. Accordingly, in their pronouncements on other religions they tended to caricature them. The influence of these caricatures sometimes pervaded their portrayal of Hinduism very substantially. This was especially true of their examination of Islam and Christianity, where the doctrinal core of these faiths was often confused with their historical role in India. Islam and Christianity, for instance, were viewed as faiths that had combined faith and conquest in considerable measure. India's slavery in their hands was deduced to a lack of such a combination. Attempts, therefore, had to be made in order to render Hinduism more militant.

Victimhood, conspiracy theories, and a never-ending sense of threat to Hinduism, which was equated with the nation, or, at least forming the very core of the nation, is the fourth element that propels this world-view. The world was divided neatly between a set of friends and a set of foes. Hinduism had to guard against the foes all the time. Enemies of the faith could come in numerous guises and disguises: Westernization, pan-Islamism, Buddhism, folk and tribal gods and goddesses, missionaries, conversion, lifestyles, heterodox ideas, scriptural interpretations, modern Indian languages, new sects, creative literature, poetry, sexual mores. The list could be endless. Why were new sects and modern Indian languages perceived as threats? New sects meant dissolving the doctrinal unity of Hinduism, which was circumscribed by the Vedas. Modern Indian languages represented newer and fresher ways of looking at the world and expressing local and folk aspirations. This militated against the Sanskritic/Brahminic tradition that the four thinkers wanted to revive. To protect Hinduism by constantly creating in-groups and out-groups, those who belong and conform, and those who do not, was of utmost importance. Those who did not fall in line had to be marginalized, ignored, harassed, and if the need arose, even eliminated.

A fifth feature of this ideal was the end of theology.[7] Hinduism had been perfected in the Vedas and the Upanishads. The question of discussing doctrinal issues, therefore, did not arise. Answers to every question about modern life, science and technology were to be found in the Vedas. The puranas had to be rejected as a mass of superstition. The Bhakti movement had to be rejected as well. One could selectively look at Bhakti poets so long as they helped in making Hindus manly and contributed to the vision of a strong, militant Hindu nation. The important thing was to return to the essential core of the Vedas and recreate a Golden Age. Everything else that followed the Vedas and the Upanishads was seen as a deviation from this precious legacy. The Vedas were the orthodox texts of the Hindus; everything else was heterodox. Losing sight of them was to forget one's orgins and deny one's patrimony.

The sixth, and last, characteristic of this ideal is the introduction of invective, abuse and contempt as legitimate tools of writing, conversation and public discourse. There was no lightness of touch in dealing with real and imagined adversaries. The truth, as the thinkers saw it, had to be told and told harshly. No concession to lack of knowledge or to emotion had to be granted. Everything had to be stripped to its basics and presented. History was a burden because it presented a picture of diversity and plurality. It allowed for language to accumulate multiple meanings. Polite words and genteel conversation was for the weak, and later, for Congressmen. These represented a departure from an unencumbered, idyllic world where things could be said directly and without the baggage of civilizational constraints. If the unpleasant truth hurt, so be it. Prophets could not make concessions to context, feelings and pragmatism. In the task of creating a Hindu nation, there was little scope for moderation and compromise.

The question of Hindu identity, then, is not one between the men of darkness and the men of light. But when the search for a rigid, ossified and regimented Hindu identity manifests as Hindutva and takes on the garb of an inflamed hypernationalism, the moment to question pieties and well-worn clichés arrives. In this sense, it is not sufficient to assume that thinkers like Gandhi and Tagore could act as antidotes to Hindutva and the politics it represents. It is true that Gandhi, Tagore, Lohia and Ambedkar refused to partake of any of the six characteristics of Hindutva discussed above. For them, identity was not a rigid, ossified and regimented entity. Rather, it was a set of flowing currents, not a fixed place or a set of stable objects.[8] For them, it was possible to have multiple identities and also actively aspire towards acquiring these multiple identities. It was important for them to celebrate their roots, their culture and a sense of belonging to the idea of India, but it was equally essential to reach out to others in order to understand, assimilate and even love them. Self-understanding was possible only when one had the ability to make place for those who were alien, different and hostile. This is where they differed from the theorists of Hindutva. Equally true is the fact that Gandhi and Tagore differed radically on issues ranging from nationalism, modernity, identity, culture and spirituality. Far more serious is the challenge that

Ambedkar posed in the form of his critique of Hinduism and of Gandhi, a challenge that is only now beginning to be taken seriously in intellectual and scholarly circles. These debates are an integral part of the larger debate on Hindu identity and its politics. What they certainly are not a part of is the dominant manifestation of Hinduism and Hindu identity in our times, namely, Hindutva.

A question is often asked: why only Hindu identity and Hindutva? Why not Islam and Christianity? After all, there is much to comment on the limitations of other faiths as well. To borrow from David Shulman's classic, *Dark Hope*,[9] one can only say that my concern in these pages is with the darkness on my side. Shulman agrees with the Greek poet Seferis who said, 'There are always but two parties – Socrates, and his accusers', and asks us to choose between these two. Having experienced the intolerance, violence, threats, domination, coercion, self-righteousness and self-serving theories of victimhood of Hindutva votaries and Hindutva politics, I, too, have made a choice. But as it was said above, Hindutva is only a means of interrogating the larger and deeper questions of Hinduism and Hindu identity, not the reason to do so.

DAYANANDA SARASWATI

Swami Dayananda Saraswati was a nationalist and a reformer of Hinduism. The introduction to his influential text, *Satyarthaprakash, The Light of Truth,* clearly delineates Dayananda's agenda, which was to bring to light 'the true meaning of truth',[1] to separate truth from falsehood, to state and write about a thing as it is. Hinduism in its Vedic formulation possessed the light of truth. The Puranas and the rise of a whole constellation of sects had eclipsed that essential truth. For India to regain its glory, it was essential to clear the fog created by the Vama Margis, the Shaivites, the Vaishnavites and several other sects and restore the pristine light of truth that emanated from the Vedas.

Why did Dayananda want to reform Hinduism and Indian society? Some insights into this quest are to be found in the image of India that was popular in the seventeenth and eighteenth centuries in the West. This perception was based largely on the imaginative reconstruction of the Orient in general, and India in particular, in literature and mythic accounts of travellers. India was seen as vulgar, sensuous, bombastic and despotic. The vast number of journals, histories, narratives, memoirs and communications concerning India from this period provided the material for the construction of such a stagnant and benighted image of India.

The Western Indologists consolidated India's image as despotic. This is the first, and most important, theme that permeated the work of nearly all Indologists during the eighteenth and nineteenth centuries. The reasons provided for existence of despotism in India varied with each Indologist, often reflecting the prevailing intellectual fashions of the day. In spite of his praise for Indian philosophy and literature of antiquity, Sir William Jones, considered the father of Indology, found India deficient in appreciation of the virtue of freedom. Despotism had made Indians insensitive to higher virtues like freedom, he claimed. He sought to make British rule in India a kind of enlightened despotism by selectively applying certain Whig principles.[2] This assertion about Indian insensitivity to freedom was extended to claim European superiority over Indians. It also acted as a catalyst for reform, as we shall see in the case of Dayananda in subsequent sections.

Indologists were classicists. The neo-classicism of the eighteenth century was permeated by a spirit of uniformitarianism which held universality, say of reason, to be the ultimate criterion of truth. The history of mankind was seen as a change for the worse; all history was an obfuscation of the real truth which was to be found in ancient times among 'savages'. If a man was by nature reasonable, then this reason was universal and uniform in all men. This world view was extended to include matters of scholarship and aesthetics. To arrive at a universally valid standard of taste, one had to read the classics. The classics were untainted by prejudice and social conventions. Following from this, the Indologists projected a highly romanticized vision of Indian society highlighted by the simple life, mysticism and harmony between man and nature. India was also seen as providing an almost unbroken tradition going back a few thousand years: in that sense it was taken to be a picture of living antiquity.

The implications of this view are complicated. At one level, the Indologists with their preoccupation with the classical and the primitive exalted ancient Indian civilization. This celebration was highly selective. William Jones, for example, while gushing over the simple life portrayed in *Abhijnana Shakuntalam,* rejected Indian spiritual life as irrational. However, at another level, most Indologists did not abandon claims of European superiority over Indians. The contribution of the Indians was in the realm of imagination. In matters of reason and taste Europeans excelled and, hence, were superior to Indians. Further, all Indologists showed little interest in contemporary India. From the perspective of these classicists, contemporary India had lost track of its ancient ideals and was in a state of utter degeneration. Indologists like William Jones felt that contemporary India was in urgent need of help. Help was to come, firstly, in the form of the new knowledge of science that Europe had recently discovered; secondly, on the cultural front, by making Indians aware of their great past.

There were others who shared the view that history was not after all the story of a steady decline, but of inevitable progress. But, they too rejected contemporary India. Their model was one of European superiority and its attendant optimism. India was seen to have contributed in the distant past to human evolution. A whole tradition of German Indologists like Herder, Schlegal and Max Mueller contributed to this theory. Hegel's views on India reflected the same trend.

A very important concern of the Indologists was religion. The attempts of Indologists to understand Hinduism were severely marred by the lack of a perspective other than that of Christianity. All Indologists acknowledged the prior claims of Christian revelation and the overall superiority of Christianity. A large part of Hindu tradition was seen to be superstitious, barbarous and savage.

The discovery of India and its historical past had provided the European mind with a new sense of chronology and yardstick of antiquity. Some like Voltaire used this to belittle the exclusive claims of Christianity. But most Indologists strove to bring Hinduism in line with the Biblical tradition and achieve a vindication of the Mosaic history. William Jones did not hesitate in distorting Hindu chronology to accommodate and bring Hinduism into the fold of the Old Testament dating.

There were the missionaries who resented the researches of the Indologists. They rejected the idea held by the likes of Warren Hastings and William Jones that Indians should be ruled according to the laws of their indigenous tradition. Charles Grant, who belonged to the Clapham sect, argued passionately for large-scale proselytizing of Hindus. Hindu religion to him was degrading. It was a violation of Christian spirit to tolerate such a religion.[3] William Wilberforce felt that Hinduism was so rotten that it was beyond the scope of reform. The only way to ensure the happiness of the British subjects of India was to convert them to Christianity.

Hinduism, then, was used not only to indicate the religion of the Hindus; it became the shorthand symbol for the West's comprehensive reaction to Indian civilization. The positing of a Hindu Golden Age was thus used to create afresh a Hinduism that was monotheistic, egalitarian, non-sectarian and non-idolatrous. Any subsequent development in Hinduism, say the Bhakti movement, was considered as a deviation from the grand ideals exemplified in the Golden Age of Vedic India. This definition and restatement of Hinduism was a result of constant criticism by missionaries and the quest of the Indologists to fit Hinduism to the model of Semitic religions.

Most times the selection of Hindu texts for study by Indologists served the purpose of colonial administration. Textual exposition of law, for instance, of the *Manusmriti*, was taken to be descriptive of reality. Legal form was given to what was social observance and customary law. The offshoot of this practice was the transformation it wrought in Hinduism. Hinduism, thus restated, tended to seek historicity for the incarnation of its deities, rejected them as deities if such historicity could not be proved, encouraged a centrally sacred book, claimed monotheism as the only valid principle of Godhead, and supported the ideal of authority of an ecclesiastical organization, supporting missionary work and conversion.

The arguments of the Indologists were used as part of the nationalist discourse in India. These statements provided Indian nationalists and religious reformers with the notion of a purified tradition that would also help them in consolidating India as a nation. The Indologists provided them with a certain self-understanding. Religious reformers reacted to their own society, culture and religion on the basis of this self-understanding. Dayananda was singularly influenced by the West's perception of India and Hinduism. *Satyarthaprakash* is a reaction to 'what others say' about Hinduism and India.

II

Dayananda wanted to bring to light the truth as it was. This truth was not a limited, localized or partial truth; it was the highest truth. What were the characteristics of this truth? To begin with, it was free of error and falsehood. Search for truth also invariably revealed the reasons for error—it could be obstinacy, wrong-headedness, wrong motives or just plain ignorance.[4] Once truth was discovered, internalized and accepted, the light of truth engulfed not only one's own faith but also all other faiths. Dayananda's mission, therefore, was to reveal the truth inherent in his faith, reject falsehoods in his own faith, and then, treat all other faiths in a similar manner:

> Despite the fact that I was born in Aryavarta, and I live there, I am not partial to the falsehoods of several sects and religious persuasions of my country. I state these falsehoods as they are and bring these to light. I treat faiths from other countries similarly. The way I speak

> to my countrymen about the progress and excellence of mankind, similarly I speak to the followers of foreign faiths.[5]

In other words, Dayananda was driving home the point that he was not partial to his faith, unlike the Christians and the Muslims, who adore, discuss and propagate their own faith while criticizing other faiths. He goes to the extent of saying that the very act of praising one's own faith, showing it in a better light and propagating it at the cost of other faiths is beyond the pale of what can be called human. In fact, the one who does is an animal. Dayananda, having stated his point clearly, goes on to overstate it. He calls individuals who are partial to their own religion not merely animals but worse than animals. What could be worse than animals? Dayananda finds such a person to be 'the older brother of animals'.[6]

Having said so, Dayananda moves on to explain the methodology of *Satyarthaprakash*:

> — Whatever truth has been published in *Satyarthaprakash* and in the ensuing chapters is appropriate in the light of the Vedas. I believe in these truths only because these have been approved in the light of the Vedas;
>
> — The new ideas of the puranas and tantras have been rejected and refuted and these are worthy of rejection;
>
> — The atheism of the Charavaks, Buddhists and Jains is discussed;
>
> — People belonging to various sects—their mind is clouded by the compulsions of their sects and their mind gets enveloped in darkness and is destroyed. I

> first look at the merits in the puranas, the Jain texts, the Bible and the Qur'an, absorb these merits and then reject the demerits. Just as I do this for the betterment of all humanity, similarly, others should do as well;
>
> — This is because it is against the grain of the wise to make people become antagonistic and come into conflict with each other because of falsehoods and because of misleading people.[7]

Dayananda's methodology offers an interesting parallel with what the French philosopher René Descartes set out to do in his *Discourse on Method*. Here is a summary of Descartes's methodology, summarized by Spinoza, an equally distinguished philosopher:

> — To set aside all prejudices.
>
> — To find the foundations upon which everything else might be erected.
>
> — To reveal the cause of error.
>
> — To understand all things clearly and distinctly.[8]

The parallels with Descartes are not limited to similarities in methodology alone. Like Descartes, Dayananda begins his search for the light of truth with the question of God and the 'idea' of God. It is noteworthy that the agenda set by the West and by Western perceptions of India strongly influenced the task of reformulating and restating Hinduism in nineteenth-century India.

Having set out his methodology, Dayananda perceived the definition of his idea of God as the most crucial task. Everything else depended on a clear and unambiguous exposition of this idea. In his view, God has to be an abstract, non-material entity.[9] The moment one spoke about terms such as 'created', 'protected', 'sustained', 'disintegrated', 'finite' and 'visible', any idea of God got nullified. God could not be subjected to the contingent and the finite. Only words like 'omniscient', 'omnipotent', 'truth', 'justice' and 'mercy' signified God. In other words, attributes such as desires, passions, pain, pleasure, finite knowledge and activity belong to the soul, not God. Further, words such as 'created', 'dissolved', 'dead', 'inert' belong to the realm of material objects, just as entities like the earth and the sun do. Dayananda wants to establish that the infinite powers and attributes of God outstrip that of matter and the soul.[10]

> A thing that is true and real, has nature, attributes and characteristics also true and real. It behoves, therefore, all men to worship and adore God and God only, none besides Him, because, even the men of yore, saints or sinners as Brahma, Vishnu, Mahadeva, Daitya, Danava, believed in and worshipped Him and Him only. They adored no other God.[11]

In short, Dayananda emphatically rejected the existence of many gods.

In order to prove the existence of one supreme God, Dayananda seeks support of the Vedas. He quotes the Yajur Veda where God is described as follows in a verse:

> By One Supreme Ruler is the whole universe pervaded, even every world in the whole circle of nature, He is the true God.[12]

Why are we to believe that what the Vedas say about God is authentic? The answer to this question is the very foundation upon which Dayananda's restatement of Hinduism rests.

First and foremost, Dayananda pronounces the Vedas to be divine in origin.[13] All other texts, without exception, had to conform to the letter and spirit of the Vedas. If they went contrary to the Vedas, they had to be rejected. The fact of the divine origins of the Vedas also rested on the fact that they were free of error and axiomatic. That is to say, the Vedas were their own authority. This was unlike other texts that were dependent on the Vedas for their authority. Interestingly, at this juncture, Dayananda lists texts that were 'snares'[14] and had to be rejected. The list includes the *Raghuvamsha, Yogavashista, Bhagavat* and *Tulsi Ramayan,* These texts have to be rejected because they contained a 'sprinkling of truth mixed with a large amount of rubbish, myths and fabrications'.[15] Till this stage, faith in the divine nature of the Vedas is just that: an article of faith. Dayananda describes this faith in the following manner:

> We believe that the Vedas alone are the supreme authority in the ascertainment of true religion—the true conduct of life. Whatever is enjoined by the Vedas we hold to be right; whilst whatever is condemned by them we believe to be wrong. Therefore, we say that our religion is Vedic. All men, especially the Aryas, should believe in the Vedas and thereby cultivate unity in religion.[16]

The Vedas were not merely religious texts. Their supremacy was instrumental in determining what constitutes 'true' religion. In Dayananda's case, his religion was the Vedic religion. He believed in it and expected all Hindus to believe in their authority. Fidelity to the Vedas was also a way of uniting the various strands of Hinduism.

A statement of faith in the Vedas still left the question of their divine origins unanswered. A minor quibble, however, had to be first got out of the way before dealing with the question of the Vedas' divine origins. Why did God decide to reveal the Vedas in Sanskrit and no other language? Dayananda said that Sanskrit belonged to no country in particular but was the mother of all languages. This still does not prove that the Vedas are of divine origin and not the work of a man. Dayananda's success in proving this would pave the way for him to reject the gods and texts of all other religions as limited, localized and of human form and invention. This is how Dayananda argued in favour of the divine origins of the Vedas:

> The book in which God is described as He is, viz., Holy, Omniscient, Pure in nature, character and attributes, Just, Merciful, etc., and in which nothing is said that is opposed to the laws of nature, reason, the evidence of direct cognizance, etc., the teachings of the highly learned altruistic teachers of humanity (Aptas), and the intuition of pure souls, and in which the laws, nature and properties of matter and the soul are propounded as they are to be inferred from the order of nature as fixed by God, is the book of Divine revelation. Now the Vedas alone fulfil all the above conditions, hence

> they are the revealed books and not books, like the Bible and the Qoran ...'[17]

The formula was very straightforward: God is eternal, and hence his knowledge was eternal. The Vedas were God's word and, therefore, they were eternal too.

Dayananda's definition of God and of the Vedas had a direct bearing on the way he perceived Hinduism and its various sects. The first casualty of this redefinition was his debunking of the incarnation theory. For Hindus to this day, faith in incarnation forms the very basis of their faith. Dayananda rejected this in totality. God, he insisted, does not incarnate. Why was this so? The Yajur Veda decreed that God is unborn and takes no human form.[18] Hence the question of incarnation did not arise. What about Krishna's promise about taking a human form whenever there was a degeneration and decay of virtue? Dayananda's answer was unambiguous:

> Being opposed to the Veda, it cannot be held to be an authority. Though it is possible that Sri Krishna, being very virtuous and being extremely anxious to further the cause of righteousness, might have wished that he would like to be born again and again at different times to protect the good and punish the wicked. If such was the case, there is no harm in it; because whatever the good and the great possess—their wealth, their bodies, aye even their hearts—is at the service of humanity. In spite of all this, Sri Krishna could never be God.[19]

God was powerful enough to save his devotees anyway. He did not need to assume the human form in order to ensure their salvation. To admit that Krishna was an incarnation would also be an affirmation of the status of Christ and many other prophets as incarnations of God. Dayananda would have none of this.

The combination of a particular notion of God and the Vedas was not merely a theological exercise. For Dayananda, the exercise of positing the Vedic religion as the only true and authentic religion had profound nationalistic overtones. It helped him, first, to create the picture of a Golden Age. Secondly, it enabled him to explain India's degeneration and its slavery as a fall from this idyllic state. Lastly, it pointed towards a solution for India's pitiful situation.

As foundation myths go, the one Dayananda created for India was at once dazzling and original. The first man, he asserts, was created in Trivishtap, what now is called Tibet.[20] At that early stage, there was only one class of human beings; that subsequently got divided into two. The good were known as the Aryas and the wicked were called Dasyus. The Aryas came down at some point and colonized the country that we now know as Aryavarta. Dayananda rejected the idea of any aboriginal inhabitants of the country, or that the Aryans came from Iran or central Asia. A most evocative description of the division of the world ensues:

> The people living in the north-east, north, north-west and west of Aryavarta were called Dasyus, Asuras and Mllechhas, while those living in the south, south-east and south-west were called Rakshasas. You can still see that the description of Rakshasas given therein tallies

> with the ugly appearance of the Negroes of today. The people living in the antipodes of Aryavarta were called Nagas, and their country Patala because of being situated under the feet (of those living in Aryavarta) ... From the time of Ikshvaku to that of Kauravas and Pandavas, the Aryas were the sovereign rulers of the whole earth, and the Vedas were preached and taught more or less even in countries other than Aryavarta.[21]

The claim of the Aryas ruling the world was a serious one. It served the purpose of glorifying the Aryas as well as striking at the belief current during Dayananda's time that going beyond the shores of India meant a loss of caste and character.

A truthful and virtuous man would remain one, said Dayananda, no matter where he is located. The ancients understood this perfectly well. After all, Patala was America in the ancient lingo and Harivarsha (literally, the abode of monkeys, because of the red lips and brown eyes of the Europeans) was Europe. Dayananda wanted Indians to go abroad for trade, travel, art, and for extending their influence over other countries. Indians also ought to associate with noble men of all countries. Dayananda suggested that the priests wanted to keep a check on travel abroad because they feared that their monopoly would be threatened as a consequence of people becoming enlightened. Look at the ancients, says Dayananda, they even formed matrimonial alliances with foreigners. Arjuna was married to Princess Ulopi of Patala, the modern-day America. They also travelled extensively:

> Krishna and Arjuna went to America in an Ashwatari vessel (i.e., one propelled by electricity) and brought

> the sage Uddalaka back with them on the occasion of the Rajasuya Yajna of Emperor Yudhisthira.[22]

This was the ancient spirit of the Vedic religion. Indians had lost sight of this and had fallen on bad times.

There were reasons, reasons that brought an end to the glorious rule of the Aryas. Dayananda lists them with great clarity:

> — Dissensions among themselves;
> — The rule of the proud, the unjust and the ignorant cannot last long;
> — Accumulation of excessive wealth in a community brings about indolence, jealousy, mutual hatred, lustfulness, luxury and neglect of duty;
> — Sound learning and education is usurped by evil customs, manners and practices like meat-eating, child marriage and licentiousness;
> — Brahmins in Aryavarta lost all learning and knowledge;
> — They could not teach the other three castes;
> — The ignorant became the teachers of people, and hence, deceitfulness, fraud, hypocrisy and irreligion began to increase among the Aryas.[23]

Dayananda's nationalistic and religious agenda is reflected in the reasons given above. It is delineated more forcefully when he says:

> It is extremely difficult for people to make any progress as long as their religion and their interests are not the same. Again they cannot progress when they do not rejoice in each other's joys, nor sympathise in each other's afflictions. But mere dining together can never

> lead to any real progress. As long as they do not avoid evil things—manners, customs, etc.,—and embrace good things, instead of making any progress they will go from bad to worse. The causes of foreign rule in India are: mutual feud, differences in religion, want of purity in life, lack of education, child-marriage, marriage in which the contracting parties have no voice in the selection of their life-partners, indulgence in carnal gratification, untruthfulness and other evil habits, the neglect of the study of the Veda, and other malpractices.[24]

Several themes are thrown up here. The allusion to 'dining together' concerns Dayananda's preoccupation with caste, whereas reference to differences in religion relates to his views on the various sects in India and their mutual antagonism. These will be discussed below in some detail.

Before taking up these themes, it is important to note that Dayananda was singularly preoccupied with politics as well. There is an entire chapter in *Satyarthaprakash* on Raja Dharma.[25] This preoccupation with politics, or more correctly speaking, the ideal mode of governance, also arises from Dayananda's analysis of the causes of India's degeneration:

> At the present moment, let alone governing foreign countries, the Aryas through indolence, negligence and mutual discord and ill-luck do not possess a free, independent, uninterrupted and fearless rule even over their own country. Whatsoever rule is left to them is being crushed under the heel of the foreigner. There are only a few independent states left. When a country falls upon evil days, the natives have to bear untold misery

> and suffering. Say what you will, the indigenous native rule is by far the best. A foreign government, perfectly free from religious prejudices, impartial towards all—the natives and the foreigners—kind, beneficent and just to the natives like their parents though it may be, can never render the people perfectly happy. It is extremely difficult to do away with differences in language, religion, education, customs and manners, but without doing that the people can never fully effect mutual good and accomplish their object. It behoves all good people to hold in due respect the teachings of the Veda and Shastras and ancient history.[26]

Self-determination, nationality as well as ethnic and racial homogeneity formed a very important part of Dayananda's political agenda.

The inspiration for this agenda, however, lay elsewhere, in Dayananda's recognition of the reasons for the advancement of Europeans. Mirroring his own political and religious preoccupations, the twelve reasons he identified constituted the basis on which Dayananda sought to 'reform' Hinduism.

1. The custom of child-marriage does not prevail among them.
2. They give their boys and girls sound training and education.
3. They choose their own life-partners. Such marriages are called Swayamvara.
4. They do not allow their children to consort with bad people. Being well-educated, they do not fall into the snares of any unprincipled person.

5. Whatever they do, they do after discussing it thoroughly among themselves and referring it to their representative assemblies.
6. They sacrifice everything, their wealth, their hearts, aye their very lives, for the good of the nation.
7. They are not indolent. On the contrary, they live active lives.
8. They allow boots and shoes made in their country to be taken in courts and offices, but never Indian shoes. This must suffice to convince you that they value their boots much more than they do the natives of many other countries.
9. They have been in this country for more than one hundred years, and yet they wear thick clothing, as they are used to at home, up to this day. They have not changed the fashion of their country, but many among you have copied their dress. This shows that you are foolish, while they are wise. No wise man will ever imitate others blindly.
10. Everyone among them does his duty most faithfully.
11. They always obey the orders of their superiors.
12. They help their countrymen in trade, etc.[27]

These are sterling qualities and noble deeds, gushes Dayananda, that have helped the Europeans to achieve unparalleled success and progress. Indians had to shed a lot of baggage and begin afresh. They had to retrieve their lost glory through recapturing the letter and spirit of the Vedas and move on to a better future on the basis of a firm commitment to the Vedic religion.

III

Dayananda's Vedic religion—he preferred to call it Vedic religion instead of Hinduism—was one of exclusion. Sects as well as other schools of philosophy had to conform strictly to Dayananda's interpretation of the Vedas. If they failed to do so, they were subjected to scrutiny and criticism. While his vision might have been to unite Hinduism under the authority of the Vedas, what he proposed eliminated the possibility of a pluralistic model of Hinduism. Non-adherence and dissent invited exclusion, at least in theory (Jihadi Hindutva has a similar agenda in contemporary India and uses similar arguments for exclusion of elements within Hinduism who dare to dissent).

The eleventh chapter of *Satyarthaprakash* is titled 'An Examination of the Different Religions prevailing in Aryavarta'. It begins by stating that there was no country in the world that could equal Aryavarta in excellence. It was a golden land, metaphorically, as well as literally. Mutual dissension, the rise of the proud, the unjust and the ignorant brought about its downfall. Increasing wealth in the antiquity brought about its attendant evils: indolence, jealousy, lustfulness and neglect of duty. This gave rise to a set of degenerate Brahmins who wanted to maintain their power and control over people.

Dayananda calls them 'popes'. What is a pope in the sense Dayananda uses the term? A 'pope' is one who robs through fraud and hypocrisy to achieve a selfish end.[28] Europe had got rid of popish practices through education and enlightenment, but India continued to be ensnared by such practices. Popery, argues Dayananda, appears in a thousand forms and guises. Its net result, however, is hypocrisy and fraud. The Vedic religion, says Dayananda, increasingly began being identified with such popish practices—feeding priests to satisfy the spirits of the dead was one such practice. A reaction to this appeared in the form of 'a most dreadful religion, called Jainism or Buddhism, that reviled the Vedas and the Shastras'.[29]

Dayananda never made a distinction between Jainism and Buddhism and found them to be one and the same, using the term 'Jain' to signify both. Jainism equated the popish practices to the Vedas. According to him, the Jains were ignorant of the Vedas and could not distinguish between their true essence and the deviant practices the degenerate Brahmins justified in the name of the Vedas. A direct and adverse consequence for Hinduism because of the Jains gaining influence was the reviling of the shastras, abandoning the custom of wearing the sacred thread, abolishing the system of brahmacharya, the mandatory period for men and women of learning and abstinence, and destruction of books of Vedic literature.

The Jains also introduced idolatry in India. They made huge statues of their religious teachers, the tirthankars, and began to worship them. Idolatry led to a decline in belief in God. The Adi Shankara eventually defeated the Jains in a religious discussion and re-established Vedic religion in India. Shankara also refuted Shaivism and the Vama Margis, followers of tantric practices. Philosophically, Dayananda had little sympathy with Shankara, but took a generous view of his philosophy. This was because he felt that Shankara might have uttered several untruths in order to defeat the Jains. Pragmatism could have impelled him to articulate reality differently, whether it was the nature of God, or of Atman and Brahman. In the context of Shankara's duel with the Jains, says Dayananda, it was understandable that he had to resort to distorting the truth; taken in itself, Shankara's philosophy was replete with falsehoods.

At this point, Dayananda undertakes a vitriolic and unsparing examination of all sects found in Aryavarta. Shaivism and the Vama Margis combined together and introduced the worship of male and female reproductive organs, the linga and the jaladhari. Dayananda calls them 'unblushing wretches'[30] who were not ashamed of following such 'idiotic practices'.[31] Skulls, stones and reproductive organs began being worshipped as a means to attain both material and spiritual ends. In his eyes, the Vaishnavites were no better. Their founder, Shathakopa, says Dayananda, was the son of a professional prostitute. His successor, Munivahana, was the son of a scavenger, who was succeeded by Yavanacharya, a man born in a Muslim family.[32] Ramanuja, who was the fourth in the line of succession, was a Brahmin, and was the one who propagated the Vaishnava creed in a systematic fashion.

Jains, Buddhists, Shaivites and Vaishnavites completely perverted the Vedic idea of an abstract, omniscient, omnipotent and all-merciful God. Instead, they introduced diabolical practices in the name of Vedic religion.

> Now if the wearing of the stones of a fruit and the besmearing of the body with ashes can lead to salvation, why then the donkeys and pigs and other animals who

> wallow in dust, and Bhils and other low-born men who wear strings of fruit-stones on their bodies [must be] already saved.[33]

Only savages, argues Dayananda, would wear rudraksha, tulsi, lotus buds, blades of grass, sandal and cover their bodies with ashes.[34] And the savages are only a little better than beasts. To believe in the efficacy of marking the forehead with a sign, tilak, to wear a rosary, to worship idols, to blow conches, to ring bells, to offer flowers, burn incense, apply sandalwood paste—all these are a denial of the freedom of will and a denial of God. These practices and observances had no sanction, whatsoever, in the Vedas.

Of all the evils that popish practices introduced in society, says Dayananda, nothing was more pernicious than idol worship. He began with a factual indictment of idol worshippers, especially the Jains and the Vaishnavites:

> The Jain idols were always naked and represented a being who was seated in a contemplative mood and had renounced the world, while on the contrary the Vaishnava idols symbolized gods having by their sides goddesses, who were dressed out in fine style and excited lascivious thoughts by their lewd charms and licentious looks.[35]

At a more philosophical level, the objections against idol worship were even more serious:

> If the sight of an idol puts God in one's mind, why cannot this wonderful creation which comprehends

> the earth, water, fire, air, and vegetation and a hundred and one other things? Cannot one think of God when he looks at the earth and the mountains which are wonderfully constructed, and out of which human beings fashion idols? It is altogether wrong to say that the sight of an idol makes one think of God. This would mean that when the idol is out of sight, the devotee would not think of God, and, consequently when all alone, may succumb to the temptation of committing theft, adultery and the like sins.[36]

The Vedas contained the truth. The Puranas and the tantras were full of falsehoods, and hence, encouraged worship of idols.

Dayananda's mission was to demystify popular Hinduism completely in favour of a cerebral and formal notion of Vedic religion. Popular myths and legends were to be discarded. Faith had to be based on a solid foundation of reason as well an adherence to first principles as enunciated in the Vedas. For instance, Dayananda rubbishes the idea that Vishnu and Mahadeva killed such demons like Tripurasura. He wonders why the same gods were not equal to the challenge of the Muslim invaders. The story of destruction of the Somanatha temple invokes a similar response from Dayananda. Instead of worshipping stones, he asserts, Indians should have worshipped heroes and brave men in order to save themselves from the Muslim invasions.

In Dayananda's rogue's gallery, there was a special place for the Bhagavat Purana. He calls the writer of the Bhagavat a 'shameless creature'[37] who had no sense of shame or hesitation in writing falsehoods.

> Oh! Why did not the writers of Bhagvat and other Puranas die in their mothers' wombs or as soon as they were born? Had the people been saved from the hands of these popes, they would have been spared of the pain and suffering that they are afflicted with.[38]

Dayananda's reaction to the story of Prahlad from the Bhagavat is illustrative of his attitude towards the signs, symbols, myths and legends of popular Hinduism:

> Now, this is another yarn like the previous ones. Let a man who recites Bhagvat or hears it read be thrown down a hill; if this story be true, he should reach the bottom unhurt. But we know what will actually happen. No Narayana will come to his help, the poor man will simply he hacked to pieces. Prahalad's father sent him to school, now what wrong did he do? That boy was such an idiot that he wanted to leave off all studies and renounce the world.[39]

While Prahlad was portrayed as a mere school dropout, Dayananda reserved his strongest indictment against the portrayal of Krishna in the Bhagavat:

> [T]he author of the Bhagvat has attributed to him as many vices and sinful practices as he could. He has charged him falsely with the theft of milk, curd, and butter, etc., adultery with the female servant called Kubja, flirtation with other people's wives in the Raas mandal, and many other vices like these. After reading this account of Krishna's life, the followers of other religions speak ill of him. Had there been no Bhagvat,

> great men like Krishna would not have been wrongly lowered in the estimation of the world.[40]

Idolatry, coupled with fantastic stories from the Puranas, had made the world look unfavourably at India as a land of superstition and ignorance. The ruin of Aryavarta was due to the misdeeds of Vama Margis, idolators and believers in the Puranas. Dayananda even implicitly approved of idolators getting 'a good thrashing at the hands of iconoclasts',[41] implying the Muslim disapproval of idolatry and its history in India.

No saint or seer or prophet escaped the brunt of Dayananda's relentless criticism. Anything that did not conform to the Vedas or deviated from a fixed trajectory of Sanskrit-based Vedic and shastric knowledge was condemned. Vedic knowledge and Sanskrit learning became the immutable orthodoxy beyond which lay a sea of ignorance and darkness. Here is an example which illustrates Dayananda's single-minded pursuit of the Vedic idea, something that often produced serious errors of judgement and taste. In this instance, the object of his ire is Kabir:

> He went to a Pundit to learn Sanskrit with him, but he insulted him by saying that he would not teach a weaver. In like manner, he went to several other Pundits but no one would teach him. Thereupon, he began to compose hymns, etc., in incorrect and unidiomatic language and sing them to weavers and other low-class people to the accompaniment of a tambura. He especially spoke ill of the Vedas, the Shastras and the

> Pundits. Some ignorant persons were ensnared into his net. After his death, his followers made a great saint of him. His disciples kept on reading whatever he had composed in his lifetime.[42]

Guru Nanak fares slightly better, but only slightly. Dayananda acknowledges that Nanak's aim of saving Hindus from embracing Islam was a good one. But he too was bereft of learning—he was ignorant of the Vedas, the shastras and Sanskrit. In a remark which betrays Dayananda's incomprehension of the significance of development of modern Indian languages, he ridicules Nanak for being acquainted merely with the dialect of Punjabi villagers and having the pretensions of composing Sanskrit shlokas.[43] Sikhs, Dadupanthis, Swami Narayan, Brahmo Samaj, Prarthana Samaj—all these religions or sects or cults had deficiencies and had to save themselves by learning the Vedas and by advancing the cause of the Vedas.

Another interesting feature of the *Satyarthaprakash* is the language Dayananda sometimes uses against those whom he perceives to be against the Vedas. The Jains were usually the 'ignorant Jainees',[44] who were 'blinded by prejudice'.[45] The books of the Jains and the Buddhists were full of 'absurdities'[46] and were nothing but unbelievable 'yarn'.[47] He comes to the conclusion that the Jains—here the term is used comprehensively by Dayananda to indicate both the Jains and the Buddhists—were 'biased, perverse, wrong-headed and ignorant'.[48] Dayananda also had a selective memory about his own positions and comments. Here is an example. He quotes a passage from a Jain text, *Prakaran Ratnakar,* which goes as follows: 'It would have been very much better if the non-Jainees—the preachers of falsehood—had not been born at all or had not attained growth, even if born.'[49] Dayananda finds this attitude against non-Jains unacceptable. Yet, only a few pages earlier, he had wished the same fate for the writer of the *Bhagavat Purana*.[50]

Dayananda judged all faiths from the perspective of their validity from a Vedic standpoint. In his comments on Hinduism, he is as unsparing as he is against Christianity or Islam. In fact, he was much more disdainful of the non-Vedic accretions within Hinduism; he felt a sense of deep commitment to Hinduism. This sense of belonging encouraged him to deal with his own faith more harshly. To reform and reinstate Hinduism to its rightful place was his life's mission. As far as other religions were concerned, they were either rivals or merely irritants. Dayananda did incorporate criticism of Hinduism emerging from other faiths; but the focus had to be reforming Hinduism, and not other faiths.

There is, therefore, a strange mixture of literality, rhetoric and disdain in Dayananda's examination of Christianity and Islam. The technique of argumentation employed inevitably rubbishes the claims of other religions and ensures Dayananda's triumph. Here is an example. Dayananda selects a quote from the Old Testament, the one which states: 'And God said, Let there be light: and there was light. And God saw the light, that it was good: and God divided the light from the darkness.' Dayananda responds to these words in the following manner:

> Was the dead inert light able to hear what God said? If so, why cannot the sun, the lamp and the light of fire hear us? The light is dead and inert and therefore cannot hear anyone. Did God only after he had seen the light know that the light was good? It appears that He did not know that beforehand. Had he known it beforehand, he would not have waited till he had seen it to pronounce it good. If he did not know it beforehand he could not have been God. Hence the Bible is not the Word of God, nor is God mentioned in it as an Omniscient Being.[51]

Satyarthaprakash is replete with such examples. This is partly due to Dayananda's preoccupation with texts. Judging Hinduism and its various living manifestations from the perspective of the Vedas, he followed a similar methodology in respect to other religions as well.

Dayananda concludes that the Christian God was not omniscient, omnipotent and universal. He was a limited and localized God.[52] 'If he is indeed omniscient, why would he have created Satan,' asks Dayananda. The Christian God was, therefore, responsible for all the evil deeds of Satan.[53] Dayananda moves a step ahead. He argues that the Christian God himself was Satan because he told lies and directed others to tell lies.

> On the other hand, God told Adam and Eve a lie when he said that by eating of the tree of knowledge of good and evil, he would surely die. Since those trees were such as gave life perpetual and the knowledge of good and evil to those who ate the fruits thereof, why did God forbid them their use, but as He did it, He stands guilty of having told a lie and mislead them, as the fruit

of those trees bestowed life and knowledge upon men, not death and ignorance.[54]

The Bible, insists Dayananda, was not even the work of a learned man, leave alone the word of God. The authors of the Bible, he asserts, were savages. They had no idea of the nature of true God. The Christian God was a 'flesh-eating trickster';[55] he was hardly God and more a man.

The New Testament provoked stronger invective from Dayananda. At a superficial level, the argument was purely political. The missionaries ridiculed stories of miracles in the Puranas, so there was little reason to believe in the miracles performed by Christ.[56] It was another matter that Dayananda categorically rejected the Puranas without exception. There is, then, the predictable rejection of the claim of Christ as the Son of God.[57] In addition, Dayananda questions the very legitimacy of the Virgin Birth. He asserts, 'This story is as possible as that recorded in the puranas about Kunti being conceived of the Sun ...'[58] In short, Jesus was to be stripped of all claims to divinity, prophethood and spirituality. 'He was the son of a carpenter,' says Dayananda, 'who must have worked as one for several years. The idea of passing off as a prophet must have entered his head one day and he began to preach in a savage country.'[59] Did he preach any thing good? Dayananda concedes Christ taught a few good things; but alongside there were many bad things as well.

What were the 'bad things' that Christ preached? Dayananda felt that Christ's entire mission and in which he was successful, was to 'set men against each other and cause them to fight'. Dayananda quotes from St Matthew,

IV, 19, 20: 'And he saith unto them, Follow me, and I will make you fishers of men. And they straightway left their nets, and followed him.' Dayananda comments on the faith Jesus founded.

> ... Jesus founded his religion in order to entrap others. He wanted to accomplish his object by ensnaring others into his net like a fisherman. Is there any wonder then if Christian missionaries follow their Master in ensnaring other men into their religion?[60]

Dayananda modelled Christ in the image of the missionaries. Swami Vivekananda had at least made a distinction between the spirit of Christ and the practice of Christianity as an organized faith. Not so with Dayananda. Christianity was condemned to falsehood because it had not partaken of the light of the Vedas.

The God of the Qur'an, says Dayananda, was not very different from the God of the Bible. At the very outset, Dayananda rejects the idea that the Qur'an was the word of God. He further rejects the idea of the God of the Qur'an being merciful. Why? Because he sanctioned the killing of animals for food. Dayananda concludes that Muslims do evil deeds in the name of God.[61] The Islamic attitude to infidels is cited as another instance of the falsity of the Qur'an as the word of God.

The history of Islam in India coloured Dayananda's view of the Qur'an entirely. The Islamic attitude towards infidels remains a centrally sore point and Dayananda returned to the question repeatedly.

> You call men professing other religions infidels, while they do the same to you, and their God curses you in

> the same way. Now will you please tell us which of the two should be considered right and which wrong? On reflection it is clear that there are errors in all creeds.[62]

But God could not have enemies. The infidels were considered enemies of God. A God who had enemies was no God at all. Muslims were apologetic iconoclasts. While they condemned image worshippers elsewhere, argues Dayananda, they themselves turned towards the Kibla to worship. He called this 'image worship on a large scale'.[63] Dayananda wanted them to break the Kibla in the same manner that they would break other images.[64] The picture painted of Islam and Muslims in the *Satyarthaprakash* is one of lasciviousness, sensuality and licentiousness.[65] In particular, the Prophet's marriage and the four wives permitted by Islam came in for his fire.

It must be pointed out that Dayananda's pronouncements were sometimes based on a partial or incorrect reading of the Qur'an's verses. Apologists of Dayananda have argued that he read the Bible and the Qur'an in Hindi and Gujarati translations and hence the odd error was bound to creep into his analysis. Without questioning Dayananda's motives or compulsions, it is worth presenting a representative example of such partially cited quotes:

> Quote from the Qur'an cited in *Satyarthaprakash:* 'And fight for the cause of God against those who fight against you. And kill them wherever ye shall find them; and eject them from whatever place they have ejected you! For civil discord is worse than carnage. Fight therefore against them until there be no more civil discord.'[66]

> Original quote from the Qur'an: 'Fight for the sake of God those that fight against you, but do not attack them first. God does not love the aggressors.
>
> Slay them wherever you find them. Drive them out of the places from which they drove you. Idolatry is worse than carnage. But do not fight them within the precincts of the Holy Mosque unless they attack you there; if they attack you put them to the sword. Thus shall the unbelievers be rewarded: but if they desist, God is forgiving and merciful.
>
> Fight against them until idolatry is no more and God's religion reigns supreme. But if they desist, fight none except the evil-doers.
>
> A sacred month for a sacred month: sacred things too are subject to retaliation. If anyone attacks you, attack him as he attacked you. Have fear of God, and know that God is with the righteous.'[67] (Holy Qur'an, II, 190–94)

Dayananda's reaction to the quote is cited in *Satyarthaprakash*:

> Had not such teachings existed in the Quran, the Mohammadans would not have been so cruel to the non-Mohammadans. They have greatly sinned by slaughtering the innocent. They hold that one who does not believe in the Mohammadan religion is an infidel, and that it is better to put infidels to sword.[68]

To Dayananda the Qur'anic God was at the root of all evils. The Qur'anic God, says Dayananda, could not keep Satan in check, since he let Satan's sins go unpunished.

The Devil tempted all, and God was the tempter of the Devil. Hence, God was the greater Devil of the two.[69]

IV

Dayananda's demolition of sects and religions was a singular act of exclusion and elimination. Unlike other restatements of Hinduism, his philosophy left little room for conversation. His almost fanatical adherence to the Vedas left little room for even Hindus belonging to various sects to gain acceptance in his eyes. Dayananda did not confine himself to criticism alone. He took his critique further. Not only were the Vedas the last and final word as far as theological and doctrinal issues were concerned, they were also the final authority on how to live one's life. He constructed an elaborate code of conduct, based on his reading of the Vedas, for the upbringing and education of children, the rules to be followed by the householder, and the code of conduct for the renunciates.

An interesting element in Dayananda's philosophy is his attitude towards caste. He favoured the varna system, the fourfold division of castes into Brahmins, Kshatriyas, Vaishyas and Sudras. In the case of the Sudras, he advocated equal opportunity for their education but was against their wearing the sacred thread.[70] Sudras, he argued quoting 'several' authorities, ought to be taught all the shastras barring the Vedas as long as they are intelligent and respectable.[71] Accepting this embargo on Sudras learning the Vedas, he gave the issue a radical edge. Quoting the Yajur Veda to support his view,[72] he gave a new twist to the very definition of the idea of who is a Sudra.

> Wherever it is declared that the Shudras are debarred from the study of the Veda, the prohibition simply amounts to this: that, he that does not learn anything even after a good deal of teaching, being ignorant and destitute of understanding, is called a Shudra.[73]

Caste, therefore, had to be based on qualification, character and accomplishments. If a high-born individual did not act like one, he had to be relegated to a lower class. In other words, Dayananda rejected the idea that caste was an accident of birth.

> All individuals should be placed in different Classes according to their qualifications, accomplishments and character. By adopting this system all will advance in every respect, because the higher Classes will be in constant fear of their children being degraded to the Shudra Class, if they are not properly educated. The same fear will also make the children acquire knowledge and culture. Whilst the lower Classes will be stimulated to exert themselves for admission into the Classes above them.[74]

In short, Dayananda did not necessarily disturb the natural order of castes. He simply disengaged the question of caste from it being a privilege of birth. In his chapter on Raja Dharma in the *Satyarthaprakash*, Dayananda was clear that as far as governance was concerned, the two upper castes, Kshatriyas and Brahmins, alone could rule.

Dayananda, in fact, established a normative parity between the Brahmins and the Kshatriyas. He expected the Kshatriya rulers to be equal to the Brahmins in knowledge, culture and piety. All forms of statecraft had to be circumscribed by dharma, literally translated as rectitude, but in this case could also mean law. Dayananda envisaged a non-authoritarian, non-despotic, form of governance for the people of Aryavarta. He was against the idea of one person concentrating absolute powers in his hands. To counter such an eventuality, he proposed a balance of power between the king, the assembly, the military and the people. It would be incorrect to translate the idea of 'people' in Dayananda to mean the masses. Dayananda visualized the setting up of three assemblies—educational assembly, religious assembly and legislative assembly. These were to be elite assemblies, where men of learning, devotion and character were included, and had no place for the Sudras.[75]

Following Manu, Dayananda also supported a system of justice that sanctioned inflicting punishment on body parts of the offender, flogging and caning. Dayananda approvingly lists the body parts on which punishment could be inflicted. He quotes *Manusmriti,* VIII, 334–338, 344–347, 350, 351, 386, and endorses Manu's penal code:

> With whatever limb a man commits an offence, even that limb shall the king remove or destroy in order to set an example to others and prevent the repetition of the same crime.[76]

Practices such as these, then, are not confined merely to the Taliban or to Middle Eastern monarchies, but have been provided for in the Hindu tradition as well.

Did Dayananda believe in any form of worship at all? His fidelity to the idea of an abstract God as enunciated in the Vedas was total. He also permitted worship of five living gods: the mother, the father, the teacher, the altruistic teacher of humanity who would be learned, deeply religious and upright, and, finally, the husband's worship of the wife and the wife's worship of the husband.[77] Giving a similar reply to the question of defining a tirtha, place of pilgrimage, he admirably presented his entire world view.

> The study and teaching of the Veda and the Shastras, association with righteous men of learning, promotion of public good, righteous living, the practice of yoga, freedom from malice and hypocrisy, truthfulness in word, deed and thought, the practice of Brahmacharya, the service of one's father, mother, tutor and the learned guests, worship of God, mental tranquility, acquisition of knowledge, both material and spiritual, and of other good qualities, and the performance of such other good works are all Tirathas, as they help one to cross the ocean of misery and sorrow.[78]

The nobility of this pronouncement conceals a problem. For Dayananda, the very definition of words like 'righteous', 'noble', 'truthfulness', 'learned', 'spiritual' and 'good' was circumscribed by a rigid adherence to the Vedas. This was the only way. There was no question of even a different interpretation of the Vedas. Dayananda had discovered the light of truth in them. It was the only way out for the advancement and salvation of India and the Hindus. Dayananda founded the Arya Samaj with just that aim in mind. It had a missionary aim and a missionary zeal.

> Hence if you are anxious for the advancement of your country, you would do well to join the Arya Samaj and conduct yourself in accordance with its aims and objects. Otherwise, you will simply waste your lives and gain nothing in the end. It behoves us all to lovingly devote ourselves with all our heart, with all our wealth, and aye, even with our lives, to the good of our country, the land of our birth, the land of the products of which we have lived, the land which sustains us still and will continue to do so in the future. No other Samaj or Society can equal the Arya Samaj in its power to raise Aryavarta. It will be a very good thing, indeed, if you would all help this Samaj, as the capability of a Samaj or Society to do good depends not on any single individual, but on all the members that support it.[79]

The nineteeth- and twentieth-century restatements of Hinduism looked up to Dayananda as someone who had reinstated India's Golden Age and had defined its origins. Sri Aurobindo saw him as someone who had 'the daring conception to build on what his penetrating glance perceived in it a whole education of youth, a whole manhood and a whole nationhood'.[80] What did Dayananda's penetrating glance perceive? Aurobindo feels that Dayananda 'perceived that our true original seed was the Veda'.[81] Vivekananda admired Dayananda for trying to find a consistent theory of the Vedas based on a new interpretation of the Samhitas.[82] Notwithstanding the praise from his contemporaries, Dayananda's extreme vision of a unified, monochromatic and aggressive Hinduism is an inspiration to votaries of Hindutva today.

SRI AUROBINDO

Political Hindutva's self-perception today is one of aggression, machismo, virility and militancy. While Ayodhya and Gujarat are the laboratories where these ideals are being tried and tested with considerable success, the minds that helped produce these conceptions drew inspiration from the nineteenth- and twentieth-century attempts to redefine and restate Hinduism. A particularly influential aspect of this representation was the view of Hinduism as a 'manly' and martial faith. Swami Vivekananda, an older contemporary of Aurobindo Ghose, had formulated his celebrated credo of beef, biceps and the Bhagavadgita as the solution for the 'weakness' and 'effeminacy' of the Hindus, reflected primarily in India's slavery for several centuries. But it is Aurobindo Ghose's formulation in this regard that is considered to be the most sophisticated.

Unlike Dayananda, Vivekananda and Savarkar, certain details about the life of Aurobindo, a revolutionary nationalist and a sage, stand out. His father, Dr Krishna Dhan Ghose, studied medicine in England and returned to Calcutta as a highly anglicized gentleman. He had forbidden his three sons to have anything to do with Indian mysticism. Fearing such local 'contamination', Aurobindo was sent to England at the age of seven. Till this time, Aurobindo spoke only English and Hindustani and did not know Bengali, his mother tongue.

In England, he was placed under the charge of a Latin scholar, Rev. Drewett, who was instructed by Krishna Dhan Ghose to keep Aurobindo away from all Indians and Indian influences. Aurobindo was trained in Greek at the St Paul's School, and spent his spare time reading English poetry, literature and fiction, French literature and ancient, medieval and modern European history. He did exceptionally well in classics at King's College, Cambridge. It was here that his interest in Joan of Arc, the American Revolution and Mazzini was kindled. This was to be the catalyst that would eventually ignite his interest in India. He eventually became a member, and then secretary, of the Indian Majlis in Cambridge, and delivered several revolutionary speeches.

Just before he left England, he became a member of a secret society called the 'Lotus and Dagger', which was formed by Indian students. Aurobindo symbolically dropped his English name, Akroyd, before returning to India. He formed no attachment with England as a country; his affection for France and European thought remained strong for the rest of his life. In 1883, he returned to India to take up various positions in the erstwhile Baroda state, rising to be the vice-principal of Baroda College. It was at Baroda that Aurobindo took the first decisive steps into political life.

Initially, Aurobindo's political activity was confined to writing a series of articles for a newspaper, *Indu Prakash*, at the instance of its editor K.G. Deshpande. He also began organizing young men in Bengal in order to build an organization that could be used for future revolutionary action. Thus, he involved himself in organizing secret societies at all levels and often travelled to Bengal for the purpose. Aurobindo clearly believed in the efficacy of a violent revolution and worked towards organizing secret revolutionary activity as a preparatory stage for open revolt and insurrection.

Aurobindo left Baroda in 1905, and in 1906 became the principal of the National College in Bengal. A cult of revolutionary politics mixed with a virulent religiosity preoccupied Aurobindo in the years after leaving Baroda. He oversaw action, such as the first 'swadeshi dacoity' in 1906 and establishment of a bomb factory at Maniktala in 1908. The bomb attack on Tardivelle, the mayor of Chandernagore (now Chandannagar), in 1908 was yet another incident choreographed by him. Aurobindo's revolutionary activities came to an end with his arrest on 2 May 1908. This came about after the Kennedy murders—Kshudiram Basu and Prafulla Chaki killed two innocents instead of Kingsford, the district magistrate of Muzzafarpur. Narendranath Gossain, who had implicated Aurobindo, was assassinated in Alipore jail.

Aurobindo was lodged in Alipore jail and aquitted after a year in May 1909. The year in jail was a decisive one for him. He spent his time in jail reading the Gita and the Upanishads and claimed to have had paranormal experiences. Religion, which was earlier a handy prop for politics, became an independent guiding force for the future maharshi. Speaking about this in the third person, Aurobindo says this of his period in incarceration:

> During this period his view of life was radically changed; he had taken up Yoga with the original idea of acquiring spiritual force and energy and divine guidance for his work in life. But now the inner spiritual life and realization which had continually been increasing in magnitude and universality and assuming a larger place took him up entirely and his work became a part and result of it and besides far exceeded the service and liberation of the country and fixed itself in an aim, previously only glimpsed, which was world-wide in its bearing and concerned with the whole future of humanity.[1]

Soon after his release, in a speech at Uttarpara in May 1909, Aurobindo had this to say:

> I spoke once before with this force in me that nationalism is not politics but a religion, a creed, a faith. I say it again today, but I put it in another way. I say that it is the Sanatan Dharma which for us is nationalism. This Hindu nation was born with the Sanatan Dharma, with it it moves and with it it grows ... The Sanatan Dharma, that is nationalism.[2]

Even after his release, Aurobindo was constantly threatened with sedition, since he had taken up the publishing of two weeklies, *Karmayogin* and *Dharma*. The threat of rearrest persisted. In 1910, on having received orders 'from above', he fled to Pondicherry, a

French colony, under a false name and passport. There he started life anew as a sanyasi, a renunciate, with an equally live interest in the affairs of the world.

As a nationalist writing in 1893, Aurobindo was acutely conscious of India's status as a slave nation. As a people, Indians were weak, cowardly, selfish, hypocritical and sentimental. But genuine patriotism and an authentic national destiny were possible, argues Aurobindo, only through the revival of the Vedic institution of the fourfold order, chaturvarna, a symbolic and typical institution often misrepresented as the four castes.[3] This was so because the original organization of Indian society was based on chaturvarna. Of these four symbolic institutions, that of the Brahmin, the Kshatriya, the Vaishya and the Sudra, the Kshatriya stood for manhood, moral and physical strength; he was the key to power and ought to govern political actions.[4] Aurobindo perceived the task of reviving a sense of manhood among Indians as the way out of India's subjection.[5]

Politics was not the business of the Brahmin whose calling was renunciation. The riches and the philanthropy of the Vaishya or the humility, contentment, service and obedience of the Sudra were not the stuff of politics either. Politics was the path of positive action, pravritti marg, and was governed by the Kshatriya morality:

> Politics is the work of the Kshatriya and it is the virtues of the Kshatriya we must develop if we are to be morally fit for freedom. But the first virtue of the Kshatriya is not to bow his neck to an unjust yoke but to protect his weak and suffering countrymen

against the oppressor and welcome death in a just and righteous battle.[6]

Arjuna, the hero of the Mahabharata, who fought a strong tyrant and a confident oppressor, was the very symbol of kshatriyahood.

Aurobindo notes that even Arjuna lapsed into kripayaavistam, pity, before he fought the great and terrible war in the Mahabharata. In extolling the virtues of kshatriyahood, this 'virus' of pity had to be overcome. Krishna did exactly that in his enunciation of the Gita. Aurobindo had a similar task cut out for him. He first proceeded to draw parallels between the Kshatriya and the samurai in Japan as the very embodiment of dynamism, valour and martyrdom. This was followed by a general justification of violence as the very bulwark of progress in society. Finally, in his *Essays on the Gita*, Aurobindo provided the most systematic justification of kshatriyahood and violence in service of this principle.

In an essay titled 'The Bourgeois and the Samurai',[7] written between 1906 and 1907, Aurobindo stated that of the two nations that had come under European influence, Japan had become a great nation, while India, despite a more ancient and splendid past, remained weak and dependent. The Japanese were able to remain faithful to their ancient traditions; the dynamic spirit of the samurai was able to mould the new knowledge that came from Europe and blend it with these traditions to suit the social and political needs of the nation.

In contrast, European culture in India had a disintegrating and destructive role. India had failed to reconstruct itself and bring about a self-revival with the help of Europe's modernity. The bourgeois had impeded India's progress. The moderation, good sense, peace, orderliness and sense of stability of the bourgeois were attributes inadequate for 'great adventures, tremendous enterprises, lofty achievements, the storm and stress of mighty and eventful periods in national activity'.[8] Only heroes, martyrs, criminals, enthusiasts, degenerates, geniuses, men of exaggerated virtue, exaggerated ability and exaggerated ideas were capable of revolutionizing society and making a nation great and free. Kshatriyahood alone could make men dare and do impossible things and, in turn, produce men of extremes, men of faith, prophets, crusaders, rebels, reckless doers and desperate adventurers. The Kshatriya principle, the Indian equivalent of the samurai one, needed light, room and air.

Allied to the idea of revival of kshatriyahood was an emphatic justification of violence as a universal principle. Aurobindo was unambiguous about the role of war and destruction as the very material basis for the mental and moral existence of human beings. There is no construction, he argued, without destruction. Life is a 'constant self-feeding and devouring of other life'.[9] This Darwinian vein is further extended to explain the limitations of ahimsa, harmlessness as Aurobindo correctly translates the term, as a vehicle for social and national growth. Harmlessness gives free play to the violence perpetrated by others. For evil to perish, it is imperative that those who live by it are destroyed.

Violence, therefore, is repayment of man's debt to Rudra. Without this, the law of Vishnu—peace and well-being—is devoid of meaning and substance.[10] The spirit of violence, however, could be purified. For this, one had to return to the old Indian system where the fighting spirit of the Kshatriya was spiritualized: The Kshatriya oppressed no one and did not allow oppression. He was always governed by dharma, a code of right conduct. For him, violence was always a moral and ethical option. It was part of being masculine. Its legitimacy derived from the need to hold together society by righteous means rather than pursue selfish ends. Increasingly, Aurobindo's justification of kshatriyahood and violence began to take a religious colour:

> [B]ut even the greatest Rishis of old could not, when the Rakshasas were fierce and determined, keep up the sacrifice without calling in the bow of the Kshatriya. We should have the bow of the Kshatriya ready for use, though in the background.[11]

The core of the teaching of the Gita, Aurobindo suggests in his *Essays on the Gita*,[12] lay in following the divine life. It was a call to abandon all dharmas, sarvadharmaan, and take refuge in the Supreme. While renunciation was one way of reaching the Divine, the Gita preferred action to inaction. The first step, therefore, was Karmayoga, followed by the path of knowledge, Jnanayoga, and, finally, the path of devotion, Bhaktiyoga. No stage precludes the other but only is raised to a higher level in order to become one with the supreme divine nature.

War, destruction and violence were part of the theory of action, qualified as disinterested action, nishkamakarma. The intellectual, social, political and moral life of humans moved forward only through a struggle. Life was a battle between what exists and what seeks to exist. To privilege ahimsa, harmlessness, as the only ideal is to allow asuric, i.e., demonic, forces, to trample, destroy, break, burn and pollute all that was good and desirable. Resistance to evil was inertia, tamas, and it injured more than it saved. Hinduism, therefore, had recognized the figure of the beneficent Durga and at the same time that of 'the terrible Kali in her blood-stained dance of destruction'.[13]

But war and violence, Aurohindo recognized, could have its own perils. That is why he advocated that military obligation should be restricted to a small class of people, the Kshatriyas. Courage, disciplined force, not arbitrary power, helpfulness and chivalrous nobility was the ideal to be pursued by a Kshatriya. It was an ideal that the Gita recognized as well, when it acknowledged war as an inevitable part of human existence and yet tried to circumscribe it with a vision of ethical and spiritual advancement.

The ideal of the Kshatriya, then, was limited to a small class of people, was in place for a limited purpose and was subject to a code of personal and societal moral advancement. In proposing the revival of kshatriyahood among all Indians, at least in spirit, Aurobindo was acutely aware of the pitfalls. He realized that once the Kshatriya fulfilled his limited role, the survival of the ideal would amount to 'an unrelieved brutality of violence stripped of its ideal and constructive aspects'.[14]

These caveats apart, Aurobindo was uncompromising in celebrating the Kshatriya ideal. The aspiration for justice, righteousness and rectitude of the Kshatriya was only an *ideal* in the ancient world. Without necessarily working out its operation in the modern world, Aurobindo perceives the fighting spirit in man as part and parcel of the soul's supreme quest.

What, then, was the true object of the Kshatriyas's life and his true happiness? asked Aurobindo.[15] To battle for the right was the duty of a Kshatriya. He would have to find a cause to conquer, to die for and become a hero. The worst grief for him was loss of honour among men of courage. To deviate from battle, courage, honour, power and rule was to lower the moral standard of mankind. Arjuna had to act, he had to fight; it was something inevitable and non-negotiable. It was an imperative of his swadharma, his social duty and the very law of his being, besides a means towards knowledge that opened deeper truths. It was a duty granted to him by the Divine.

War and violence were justified by the nobility of the objective, namely, slaying asuric forces. The act of killing itself was seen as favouring the immortality of the soul. To kill asuric individuals was to prepare oneself for immortality. Moreover, since all actions were for the sake of the Divine, they were to be seen purely as acts of sacrifice undertaken without attachment or desire. Further, drawing upon the Gita, Aurobindo argued that it was the Divine who 'has already slain the Dhritarashtrians, he of whom Arjuna is only the human instrument'.[16]

This power of kshatriyahood was not beyond limits. Though Aurobindo held that the ideal of kshatriyahood (exemplified by Arjuna) was a virtue worthy of emulation in colonial India by weak and unmanly Indians, he also paid due attention to the delineation of asuric qualities among human beings. While there is scant detail in the

Essays on the Gita or other works about how this mission to impart kshatriyahood in Indians was to be actualized, Aurobindo's explanation of asuric qualities is interesting.

Asuric qualities comprised harshness, hardness, fierceness, and satisfaction in slaying enemies, amassing wealth and unjust enjoyments.[17] An asura was one whose dominant rajasic nature was 'turned towards egoistic greatness, satisfaction of desire, the indulgence of their own strong will and personality which they seek to impose on the world, not for the service of man or God, but for their own pride, glory and pleasure'.[18] Asuric nature was imbued with wrath, greed, cunning, treachery, doing wilful injury to others, pride, arrogance and excessive self-esteem. In contrast, the deva nature was characterized by self-control, sacrifice, the religious habit, cleanness and purity, candour and straightforwardness, truth, calm and self-denial, compassion to all beings, modesty, gentleness, forgiveness, patience, steadfastness, a freedom from restlessness, levity and inconstancy.[19]

In other words, the deva qualities were part of the satvic ideal. As for the asuric qualities, Aurobindo described their nature as fierce, titanic, destructive and arrogant. Adding a very important gloss on the question of asuric qualities he says,

> The Asuric Prakriti is the rajasic at its height ... [F]or the unbridled force of the rajasic nature, when exhausted, falls back into the weakness, collapse, darkness, incapacity of the worst tamasic soul-status.[20]

Rajas, it is worth recalling, was the attribute of the Kshatriya. An asura was, therefore, a Kshatriya who did not recognize any limits and was not subject to any moral law. Arjuna was of the deva nature and not the asura prakriti because God was his charioteer. He was asked by the Divine to establish the kingdom of dharma, righteousness.

In the absence, therefore, of a commonly accepted moral universe and ethical framework, kshatriyahood was bound to lapse into asuratva, demonic forces. It is interesting to note that despite a clear understanding of the asura qualities, Aurobindo did not make the connection between unbridled rajas and asura qualities. There is a clear exposition of the asuric and the rajasic qualities as independent entities. These are presented as independent, mutually exclusive, theoretical ideals by Aurobindo without a sense of the thin line that divides the two ideals in practical life. Shorn of its status as an ideal, kshatriyahood in practice could easily lapse into asura prakriti. Put differently, asuratva is 'Ksatriyahood which has run amuck'.[21]

There is ambiguity in Aurobindo's thought regarding the question of making Indians more 'manly'. There are instances where he proposes the Kshatriya ideal for curing the weaknesses and cowardice of Indians. This was part of his nationalist mission and part of his early revolutionary activities. Elsewhere, he speaks of kshatriyahood as the governing principle of politics alone. In this instance, the kshatriyahood principle is spoken of as a normative concept rather than as a practical one. What is absolutely clear, however, is that Aurobindo equated this principle with manliness.

This is yet another inversion in his thought which inaugurates a separate set of problems. In the Indian cosmology, it was the cerebral, self-denying and ascetic Brahmin who represented the masculine principle. The violent, virile and active Kshatriya, on the other hand, stood for the feminine principle. Ananda K. Coomaraswamy in his *Spiritual Authority and Temporal Power in the Indian Theory of Government* clearly says:

> [T]he King, who is unquestionably the 'feminine' party in the 'marriage' of the Sacerdotium (brahma) and the Regnun (ksatra).[22]

Coomaraswamy clarifies that the king, traditionally a Kshatriya, was feminine to the Brahmin but male to his own realm. Just as a woman was assimilated to a man, so was the Kshatriya to the Brahmin. In the *Atharvaveda Samhita,* III. 4.1, the priest tells the king: 'Bear thou rule' *(tvam vi raja). Atharvaveda Samhita,* II. 36.3 cites the instance of the same words spoken to a wife: 'Let her bear rule' *(vi rajatu).* The *Aitareya Brahmana,* III. 11 says: 'Forward the Spiritual-authority, forward the Temporal-power! Unto their Union.' Aurobindo conflated the ideals exemplified in the scriptures; the Kshatriya was a feminine principle in the marriage of the sacred realm (brahma) and the kingly realm (kshatra). This balance of the sacred and the temporal ensured clear demarcation of authority and put limits on their respective functions. It is only when the sacred and the spiritual act together that they possess the right to counsel and command the populace. In other words, the Kshatriya was meant to implement the purpose delineated by dharma, set out by the spiritual authority representing the will of God on earth.

Aurobindo perceived that his project of making Indians 'manly' was, however, impossible without the recovery of Aryan thought, discipline and character. Any national revival had to be based on retrieving the patrimony of the Aryan forefathers.[23] The Aryan protects his friends and subdues his enemies, but does so in a disinterested manner. He is neither intoxicated by victory nor does he hate his enemies. In a dramatic statement, Aurobindo puts forth the central proposition of Aryan thought:

> Narayana is everywhere, so whom shall I hate or whom shall I despise?[24]

Western philology had converted the word 'Arya' into a racial and ethnological term. In the Vedas, however, the Aryans were those who had accepted a particular form of self-culture which reflected in their inward and outward practices.[25]

In the modern context, according to Aurobindo, re-Aryanization was to be a relatively effortless activity. This was because Indians were 'men with Occidental impulses in our blood'.[26] He argued that given the light and air of the European context, Indians too could shape themselves and progress in the manner Europeans had done. Contemporary India was shallow, vain and mentally impotent. It had lost contact with Shakti, power, and had fallen into despair and had become degenerate. Oscillating between Western and Hindu thought, Aurobindo chose to define this lost power as a loss of Shakti.

All that happens in the world, holds Aurobindo, is the work of the Divine through his Shakti, who is the Divine Mother. The Mother in every age embodies a distinct principle. In the current age, the Mother made herself immanent as the Shakti of War, the Shakti of Wealth and the Shakti of Science. India crawled today because the people had abandoned Shakti and had been abandoned by Shakti.[27] The Shakti of Science was mightier than ever before.

To appropriate the Shakti of Science was to rekindle in ourselves the Arya Shaktis that were in our blood and were part of our patrimony. For this, Indians had to be made more 'manly', and kshatriyahood had to be rediscovered. European science, said Aurobindo, is the mace of Bheemsen and a weakling could not wield it.[28] To master European science, Indians had to re-Aryanize themselves. Only religion could provide the instrumentality to 'wield the stupendous weapons of western knowledge and science as lightly and invincibly as Arjun wielded the Gandiv'.[29] European science was a triumph of the man of knowledge. The only way to gain Shakti was knowledge. India's weakness was its diminution of thought power.

Kshatriyahood, manliness, Aryanization and European science were, therefore, part of the same continuum. In fact, these could be used interchangeably. As with kshatriyahood, science too could lose sight of its limited purpose and turn asuric. Aurobindo, for all his enthusiasm for European science, called it a light within a limited room, apara vidya, a lower form of knowledge. The inwardness of religion alone could triumph over the ills of science, especially materialism. While the Shakti of Science was supreme in this age, it had to contend with several mlechchha shaktis, which were clouded in tamas or darkness. These dark forces of science generated a new form of barbarism in the shape of industrialism, commercialism and materialism.

This warning against the unbridled play of science did not negate Aurobindo's enthusiasm for 'the scientific method of the adult and senescent West'.[30] India knew how to harmonize matter and spirit and would be able to bring about a synthesis of science and spirituality. Despite all such disclaimers, the burden of Aurobindo's argument remained consistent: Indians were weak and unmanly and therefore required the Kshatriya impulse; they had grown feeble and had to appropriate the Shakti of Science; to wield the Shakti of Science they had to re-Aryanize themselves; re-Aryanizing, among other things, meant a rediscovery of Occidental impulses already present in the Indian blood.

II

Kshatriyahood, re-Aryanization and the Shakti of Science were then Aurobindo's ingredients for the new nationalism. It was to be an all-encompassing ideology to bring about unity among all sections of Indian society. This new nationalism[31] was a creed, but it was more than a creed; it was a method, but more than a method. Rather, it was an attempt at the spiritual transformation of nineteenth-century India. It was a call for men 'who will dare and do impossibilities, the men of extremes, the men of faith, the prophets, the martyrs, the crusaders, the [...] rebel, the desperate adventurers and reckless doers, the initiators of revolutions'.[32] The new Nationalism was the rebirth of the Kshatriya in India.

The only qualification that this new creed demanded of its followers was a body made in the womb of an Indian mother, a heart that felt for India, a brain that thought ideas to bring about her greatness, a tongue that adored her name and hands that could quarrel on her behalf.[33] Aurobindo's conception of new Nationalism increasingly took on a highly romanticized and religious colour. Nationalism was an avatar, he argued, and cannot be slain. It was the divinely appointed shakti of the Eternal and was here to accomplish a God-given task. The task, primarily, was the passionate aspiration for the realization of an essential unity and equality in the nation; and that was nothing but the realization of divine unity.

Since the genius of Indians had poured itself into religion, the only way to generate national self-consciousness was to consider patriotism as religion. Aurobindo makes use of Bankim Chandra Chatterji's imagery of the nation as Mother. Aurobindo was deeply influenced by Bankim who had given Indians the 'reviving mantra of *Bande Mataram*'.[34] It transformed the notion of the motherland from a mere intellectual idea to an emotional and spiritual idea:

> It is not till the Motherland reveals herself to the eye of the mind as something more than a stretch of earth or a mass of individuals, it is not till she takes shape as a great Divine and Maternal Power in a form of beauty that can dominate the mind and seize the heart that these petty fears and hopes vanish in the all absorbing passion for the Mother and her service, and the patriotism that works miracles and saves a doomed nation is born.[35]

Patriotism was, thus, a national religion. Nationalism too was not a mere political programme but a religion.

New nationalism was an attempt to bring about a happy union of religion and politics. National awakening was impossible without a religious awakening. Politics too had to be based on religion. Aurobindo imparted this argument a prophetic twist when he asserted that the need was 'to recognize that politics is religion and infuse it with the spirit of religion'.[36]

Swaraj, freedom, was not, therefore, to be seen as an aspiration for political liberty alone. It was to be seen as the final fulfilment of the Vedantic ideal in politics, a realization of the ancient life of India under modern conditions, and the return to an epoch of truth and righteousness, satyayuga.[37] Only by bringing all questions of politics, society, theology, philosophy, literature and science under one national religion was true swaraj possible. This national religion had to be universal.

What was this national religion? Aurobindo is categorical that sanatana dharma, the eternal religion, could have a universal sway over all facets of life in the nation:

> There is a mighty law of life, a great principle of human evolution, a body of spiritual knowledge and experience of which India has always been destined to be guardian, exemplar and missionary. This is the sanatana dharma, the eternal religion.[38]

Spirituality, Aurobindo emphasizes, was India's only politics and the fulfilment of the sanatana dharma its only swaraj.[39] India's spiritual unity was always complete and it stretched from the Himalayas to the seas. Neither lack of national and political unity nor foreign invasions had been able to crush this cultural and spiritual unity.

In his early writings, Aurobindo thought unity of religions unnatural. Human beings differed and so there must be a plurality of religions and even different sects of the same religion.[40] The idea of an eternal, universal religion is a later development in his thought. He, however, always held the view that religion, spirituality, idealism, altruism and the quest for perfection were the collective destiny of mankind. Aurobindo makes an important distinction between true religion and religionism.[41] True religion was spirituality, which, in turn, was 'simply to keep our center, our essential way of being, our inborn nature'.[42] Spirituality rejects nothing and assimilates all that is received. Religionism was about intellectual dogmas, forms, ceremonies, rigid moral codes and religio-political and religio-social systems. Religionism is required before the lower natures of human beings can approximate to higher spiritual truths.

Hinduism was also of two kinds. Aurobindo, like all nineteenth- and twentieth-century reformers of religion, was in favour of doing away with sects and rituals. His typology of Hinduism conforms to the attempts during that period of purging religion of all popular outer forms:

> One which takes its stand on the kitchen and seeks its Paradise by cleaning the body; another which seeks God, not through the cooking pot and the social convention, but in the soul ... It is the Hinduism of Bhishma and Srikrishna, of Shankara and Chaitanya, the Hinduism which exceeds Hindusthan, was from old and will be for ever.[43]

In contemporary India, Aurobindo averred, Hindus had

replaced the superstitions of popular Hinduism by the equally debilitating superstitions of materialistic science.

The divisions within Hinduism could only be rectified through subordinating sectarian differences to a body of spiritual truths. These spiritual truths must be distinct from the spiritual truths of all other religions. All Hindus must come to a common agreement about the need to cherish Hinduism as a sacred and inalienable possession.[44] Antiquity alone could not be the sole arbiter of the usefulness of Hinduism. Every tenet had to stand the test of contributing to the nation's future. The conservative elements in Hinduism, while preserving it against foreign assault, had reduced it to a tamasic, inert, ignorant and uncreative faith.

Hinduism's basic spirit celebrated the existence of 'one invariable and indivisible divinity in every individual'.[45] It was an eternal religion as well as a universal religion that embraced all other religions. For a religion to be eternal, it had to be universal.[46] As a faith, Hinduism accepted all forms of religion because of its faith in the One; it was tolerant and simultaneously full of faith and fervour. It embraced science, faith, theism, Christianity, Islam and Buddhism. Such Hinduism was a law of life. It rejected nothing but accepted only after testing the idea's validity. Hinduism as sanatana dharma had many scriptures and yet it did not reject the truths of the Bible and the Qur'an.[47]

To reiterate: Hinduism had no dogma, no 'church', and it embraced all faiths. The truths of Hinduism permeated every single aspect of life and it set its sight towards the Infinite. It rejected nothing and was supremely tolerant. In actual practice, what did this tolerance translate into? Aurobindo affirms:

> The inner principle of Hinduism, the most tolerant and receptive of religious systems, is not sharply exclusive like the religious spirit of Christianity or Islam.[48]

In other words, Hinduism was superior but also tolerant towards what Aurobindo perceived as the flaws of other faiths.

At first sight, it seems as if Aurobindo, revolutionary, nationalist and man of religion, is merely making a case for the superiority of his faith, while admitting that from the imperium of his faith other religions may look inadequately non-dogmatic and tolerant. But Aurobindo's statement on Hinduism goes a step further:

> [Hinduism] is in the first place a non-dogmatic inclusive religion and would have taken even Islam and Christianity into itself, if they had tolerated the process.[49]

What if Islam and Christianity were to refuse to be assimilated and further refuse to acknowledge the superiority of Hinduism's claims? Aurobindo gives an early intimation of what is today unfolding as jihadi Hinduism:

> Hinduism has always been pliable and aggressive; it has thrown itself on the attacking force, carried its positions, plundered its treasures, made its own everything of value it had and ended either in wholly annexing it or driving it out by rendering its further continuation in the country purposeless and therefore impossible. Whenever it has stood on the defensive, it has contracted within narrower limits and shown temporary signs of decay.[50]

Kshatriya 'masculinity', rather than the Gandhian notions of ahimsa and self-denial would be the impulses to bring about this assimilation; it would thus be central to the very spirit of Aurobindo's interpretation of Hinduism.

III

As a revolutionary nationalist writing in the first decade of the twentieth century, Aurobindo welcomed pan-Islamism and the rise of a separate Muslim self-consciousness. He saw it as a sign of the vitality of nationalism and as part of the process of nation building. Nevertheless, he opposed the idea of separate electorates for Hindus and Muslims because this concept recognized both communities as permanently separate political units. Separate electorates that the British proposed vitiated the growth of a single, unified nation. The Hindu–Muslim problem was, according to him, a creation of the British who wanted to keep the two faiths apart.

In the arena of politics, Aurobindo was prepared to meet the Muslims in a manner chosen by them. It could take the form of 'the firm clasp of the brother or the resolute grip of the wrestler'.[51] For the larger question of Hindu–Muslim unity, Aurobindo proposed a Vedantic solution.[52] Discord between Hindus and Muslims, he felt, was the consequence of a series of misunderstandings. Love compels love and strength helps the strong to be in a position to conciliate. The Muslims ought not to be flattered, nor should they be approached with weakness and cowardice. It ought to be understood that 'in him too Narayana dwells and to him too our Mother has given a permanent place in her bosom'.[53] For better understanding and empathy, the Prophet and Islam had to be better communicated to 'us', the Hindus.

The Muslims were always a coherent and united community, bound together by the threads of equality and brotherhood. In contrast, the Hindus were flexible, progressive, elastic and intellectually and morally sensitive.[54] Apart from a spiritual impulse, the only other thing that could unite the Hindus was a need to preserve and further the goals of their community and faith. Interestingly, Aurobindo rejected the 'low' motives of the Hindu Sabha of marshalling the 'force of a united Hinduism against the intensity of a Mahomedan self-assertion'.[55]

Aurobindo began by emphatically rejecting Lala Lajpat Rai's thesis that Hindu nationalism was a precondition for the establishment of a great Indian nationality.[56] Hindu–Muslim rivalry was a fact of history but Hindu nationalism was certainly not its solution:

> Hindu nationalism had a meaning in the times of Shivaji and Ramdas, when the object of national revival was to overthrow a Mahomedan domination which, once tending to Indian unity and toleration, had become oppressive and disruptive.[57]

In modern conditions, Aurobindo felt, the basis for nationality ought to be different. He favoured the principle of swadesh, or self-ruled nation, where Hindus and Muslims live side by side.

According to Aurobindo, for Hindu nationalism to survive, geographical separateness was a must. Maharashtra and Rajasthan, which formed such a unit before the British rule came to India, were now part of a single country. The first prerequisite for Hindu nationalism, namely, a geographically and racially distinct territory, was missing.

Here Aurobindo's argument takes a strange turn. He says that Muslims saw the question of nationalism differently:

> The Mahomedans base their separateness and their refusal to regard themselves as Indians first and Mahomedans afterwards on the existence of great Mahomedan nations to which they feel themselves more akin, in spite of our common birth and blood, than to us.[58]

The Hindus, he avers, had no such choices given to them. They were bound to the soil. They could not deny their Mother.

Having begun by rejecting Hindu nationalism, and continuing that under modern conditions Hindus and Muslims had to live together in a mutually shared swadesh, Aurobindo now proposes his ideal of Indian nationalism:

> Our ideal therefore is an Indian Nationalism, largely Hindu in its spirit and traditions, because the Hindu made the land and the people and persists, by the greatness of his past, his civilization and his culture and his invincible virility, in holding it, but wide enough to include the Moslem and his culture and traditions and absorb them into itself.[59]

What if the Muslim in India refused to be absorbed? In that case, Aurobindo went on, '… the Hindu, with what little Mahomedan help he may get, must win Swaraj both for himself and the Mahomedan in spite of that resistance.'[60]

After proposing that the basis for an Indian nationalism had to be largely Hindu in spirit and the Muslims had a choice whether to join or opt out, Aurobindo, ironically, returned to the theme that the Mother should not be seen as the Mother of Hindus alone.

This shift in his view of Muslims is evident in Aurobindo after 1910, when the revolutionary nationalist had chosen to become a maharshi. While he ceased to participate in active politics, Aurobindo continued to take a lively interest in it and in the fate of India. He reacted ordinarily to political events unfolding in the country. The Hindu–Muslim question preoccupied him more than ever before. He felt that Gandhi and the Congress were making a fetish of the issue of Hindu–Muslim unity. In 1923, Aurobindo moved close to issuing the Muslims a warning:

> It is no use ignoring facts; some day the Hindus may have to fight the Muslims and they must prepare for it. Hindu–Muslim unity should not mean the subjection of the Hindus. Every time the mildness of the Hindus has given way. The best solution would be to allow the Hindus to organize themselves and the Hindu–Muslim unity would take care of itself, it would automatically solve the problem.[61]

It is this very solution that Aurobindo had rejected in 1909 as the 'low motive' of the Hindu Sabha, calling it a 'rivalry with Mahomedan pretensions'.[62]

Also in 1909, Aurobindo was finding it impossible to live amicably with a religion 'whose principle is "I will not tolerate you"'.[63] No unity was possible with people of this kind. Certainly, no talk of unity was even conceivable if the Muslims continued to convert Hindus while the Hindus could not or would not convert Muslims. The only way to make the Muslims 'harmless' was to make them lose their fanatical attachment to their religion.[64]

How far Aurobindo had moved on this issue by September 1923 can be gleaned from his pronouncements. He was now arguing that the Islamic civilization and culture 'hardly gave anything to the world which may be said to be of fundamental importance and typically its own'.[65] It was a derivative culture. No profound thoughts could be seen in their religion and philosophy, which were very simple. Their most minimal contribution to India was the introduction of Indo-Saracenic architecture. They also introduced some new forms of poetry and art. But their political institutions were always semi-barbaric. What Islam required was a transformation in its religion that would, in turn, bring about a change in the Muslim temperament.[66]

To a question in 1926 about the possibility of assimilating Muslims in India, Aurobindo answered in the affirmative but put forth a condition. No longer was there any reference to the idea of the Muslims having been given a permanent place in the Mother's bosom:

> Why not? India has assimilated elements from the Greeks, the Persians and other nations. But she assimilates only when her central truth is recognized by the other party, and even while assimilating she does it in such a way that the elements absorbed are no longer recognizable as foreign but become part of herself ... The assimilation of the Mahomedan culture was done in the mind to a great extent and it would have perhaps gone further. But in order that the process may be completed it is necessary that a change in the Mahomedan mentality should come. The conflict is in the outer life and unless the Mahomedans learn tolerance I do not think the assimilation is possible.[67]

In contrast, Aurobindo underlined, the Hindus were ready to tolerate. They were always open to new ideas and had a tremendous capacity to assimilate. All that they demanded was that their central truth be recognized.

Aurobindo was firm that nothing ought to be done to conciliate the Muslims. If the Muslims were to be placated, it would amount to abandonment of the greatness of India's past and her spirituality. By 1934, 'India' and 'Hindu' were interchangeable terms for Aurobindo. Deletion of parts of the song '*Vande Mataram*' by some Congressmen was for Aurobindo a case of asking Hindus to give up their culture.[68] The nation was the Mother. Durga had manifested in the form of the Mother. Nationalism was a religion; or rather religion was the only politics of the nation.

By 1939, Aurobindo's utterances on Hinduism and Hindus seemed to echo the notions of Hindutva that Savarkar was advocating. Absent was any idea of a liberal democratic nation, based on an impersonal and formal notion of rule of law, respect for plurality and ensuring a minimum amount of liberty for all. Rather, it was a war of incommensurable ideas of identity politics masquerading as rival notions of morality.

Aurobindo's contribution to the rise of political Hindutva is second to none. His notion of kshatriyahood has slided into asuratva, his ideals of sanatana dharma and re-Aryanization have been turned into political slogans. Religion, indeed, has become politics, perhaps the only politics we know of today. The maharshi has turned into a pamphleteer of the Hindu rashtra concept without being conscious of it:

> In the Indian conception of nationality, the Hindu view would naturally be there. If it cannot find a place there, the Hindus may as well be asked to give up their culture. The Hindus don't object to 'Allah-ho-Akbar' ...[69]

Aurobindo, in one of his mystical flights, had written that no one really knew anything about his life. It had not been on the surface for men to see, he said. His writings, however, have inspired a jihadi Hinduism and political Hindutva that might require the coming of the Shakti of Peace, the Shakti of Reason and the Shakti of Moderation to undo the damage.

SWAMI VIVEKANANDA

Political Hindutva takes on many guises and indulges in various subterfuges. The latest and most successful of these has been the creation of an entity called 'soft' Hindutva. This principle is constantly counterposed to Hindutva of the Modi, Togadia and Advani variety. Every time a place of worship is felled, each occasion when a riot breaks out, and each time the minorities are systematically persecuted, ideologues of political Hindutva strategically distance themselves from the jihadi elements and pronounce 'soft' Hindutva to be representative of 'true' Hindutva. In order to justify the claims of 'soft' Hindutva, invariably, the ideas of two icons—Swami Vivekananda and Maharshi Aurobindo—are resurrected.[1] Atal Bihari Vajpayee chose to quote Swami Vivekananda twice in his musings from Goa in December 2002. Interestingly, these musings came after the Gujarat riots and after Narendra Modi's triumph in the assembly elections subsequently.

Vivekananda lends himself readily to such indiscriminate quotation. Of all attempts at a restatement of Hinduism in the nineteenth and twentieth centuries, his is the most complex. It does not lend itself to easy generalizations nor does it afford quick solutions to ordinary existential problems. For the Swami himself, the enterprise of reinterpreting Hinduism was mediated by several factors. As a religious preacher, he had to contend with the missionaries' barbs against his faith. At the same time, aware of the limitations of the brand of Hinduism practised in his time, he took upon himself the task of rectifying what he perceived as several anomalies and deviations. He also sought to place Hinduism within the context of resurgent nationalism and sought a role for it in India's future emancipation. Lastly, there was a personal dimension to Vivekananda's project of restating Hinduism: it had to address his spiritual quest and show him the path towards his mukti or salvation that he characterized in his own unique way.

To paraphrase Nietzsche, votaries of political Hindutva behave like plundering troops: they take away a few things they can use, dirty and confound the remainder, and revile the whole. As the following pages will illustrate, Vivekananda is an inadequate model for 'soft' Hindutva. If anything, as we examine his thought, he emerges as a proponent of a strong, virile and militant ideal of the Hindu nation. (This is not an attempt to question his motives. Rather, it is to illustrate the fragility of his notions like tolerance and unity of all faiths.) More importantly, it is to show the sad trajectory of a lot of nineteenth- and twentieth-century Indian thought: its inability to transcend context and history to carve out an alternative universe, a new metaphysics.

Towards the end of his life, Swami Vivekananda did approximate to a definition of Hinduism that was sparse and unencumbered. It had very little to do with the sanctity of scriptures, places of worship or dogma, much less with any brand of identity politics. The Sangh Parivar and proponents of its brand of political Hindutva would find little use for this radical definition of Hinduism. This chapter is an attempt to map the complexities that went into Vivekananda's restatement of Hinduism.

I

On 15 February 1895, Swami Vivekananda wrote a letter from New York in the form of a poem to Mary Hale, one of the two daughters of Mr and Mrs George W. Hale. The Hale family was very close to the Swami and he addressed Mr and Mrs Hale as Father Pope and Mother Church. Two stanzas of the poem are crucial. They represent Vivekananda's self-perception as a Vedantin. This was the image of himself he liked to project and this was the goal he struggled to attain all his life. These two stanzas best represent Vivekananda's tortured quest in coming to terms with Hinduism, the philosophy of his guru, Sri Ramakrishna, and his own project of restating Hinduism:

Nor angel I, nor man, nor brute,
Nor body, mind, nor he or she,
The books do stop in wonder mute
To tell my nature; I am He.

Before the sun, the moon, the earth,
Before the stars or comets free,
Before e'en time has had its birth,
I was, I am, and I will be.[2]

It was easier to attain the lofty stance of Advaita Vedanta in verse form and say 'I am He', meaning the pure, universal spirit or soul, the Brahman, but it was certainly much more difficult to translate the concept meaningfully in practical life. Vivekananda saw Sri Ramakrishna attain the light of Vedanta in his lifetime. This impelled the former, Ramakrishna's favourite disciple, to give his guru the epithet 'Naradeva Deva'—'the God of the gods that dwells in all humans'.[3] To become a naradeva deva was Vivekananda's own aspirational universe.

Despite his unquestioned devotion to Sri Ramakrishna, Vivekananda felt that he had to work out his own method towards salvation. He was grateful to his teacher, yet he feared bondage to the guru's method of realizing the ultimate truth.[4] He worshipped his guru as God but was not prepared to follow him blindly. Vivekananda thought of his relation with Sri Ramakrishna as one that existed between Christ and Paul.[5] Sri Ramakrishna was free like Christ, but he was free in love not in 'thunder'. Sri Ramakrishna, like Christ, created, but it was the thundering sort like Paul who 'spread the light'.[6]

To become the thundering sort who would spread the light, Vivekananda had to, firstly, restate Sri Ramakrishna's mandate to him. Vivekananda sought to suggest that arriving at 'the mandate' would entail twin denials on his part. The first meant a denial of the conventional duty of a sanyasi, a renunciate. There was no question of a sanyasi 'helping' anybody. For a renunciate, the question of duty towards individuals or towards society was a superfluous one. Vivekananda stated this classical position beautifully:

> Do not create illusion by helping anyone. It is like a banyan tree that spreads on and on. If you are a dualist, you are a fool to try to help God. If you are a monist, you know that you are God; where find duty? You have no duty to husband, child, friend. Take things as they come, lie still and when your body floats, go; rise with the rising tide, fall with the falling tide.[7]

Vivekananda rejected this view of renunciation and said that the true mark of a renunciate was to help others see the truth. In order to arrive at this position, he would have to give up his own personal goal of attaining moksha or eternal freedom. This was the second denial. Again he sought legitimacy in 'the mandate' given to him by Sri Ramakrishna. One day he went into a state of samadhi—the state where the difference between the individual and the Absolute vanishes. On subsequent occasions, he failed to attain this state. He mentioned this to his guru who told him that if he remained 'day and night in this state, the work of the Divine Mother will not be accomplished; therefore you won't be able to induce that state again; when your work is finished, it will come again'.[8]

Two or three days before leaving his body, Sri Ramakrishna gave his pupil 'the mandate'. On this occasion, Vivekananda was sitting in front of Sri Ramakrishna and again fell into a state resembling samadhi. On returning to consciousness, he saw his guru weeping. This is how Vivekananda chose to describe the ensuing conversation:

> On questioning him, he answered me affectionately, 'Today, giving you my all I have become a beggar. With

> this power you are to do many works for the world's good before you will return.' I feel that that power is constantly directing me to this or that work. This body has not been made for remaining idle.[9]

In other words, the 'mandate' ensured that Vivekananda could not lie still. He had to help others, be the thundering sort, and love humanity. This direction from his guru created a tension within Vivekananda who often felt that his life's mistakes were a result of too much love and bhakti, devotion, and wished he could 'be an Advaitist, calm and heartless'.[10] Indeed, his adherence to Advaita Vedanta, or his version of it that he chose to call practical Vedanta, was also born out of this creative tension within himself and the legacy of his guru.

Sri Ramakrishna used to teach dualism—we shall, in subsequent sections, see Vivekananda unleash uncontrolled fury upon dualists whom he saw as barbarous and fanatical—and never taught Advaita. But he taught Advaita to Vivekananda, who himself was a dualist earlier.[11] Dualism for Vivekananda manifested in the form of Kali worship by Sri Ramakrishna. At one stage, Vivekananda used to hate Kali and 'all her ways'.[12] He was made to like her by Sri Ramakrishna who 'made me over to her'.[13] But Vivekananda believed in the nameless, formless, eternal Brahman of Advaita too. How were the two to be reconciled?

> You see, I cannot but believe that there is somewhere a great Power that thinks of Herself as feminine, and called Kali and Mother ... And I believe in Brahman too ... But is it not always like that? Is it not the multitude of

> cells in the body that make up the personality, the many brain-centres, not the one, that produce consciousness? ... Unity in complexity! Just so! And why should it be different with Brahman? It is Brahman. It is the One. And yet—and yet—it is the gods too![14]

This reconciliation was, however, Vivekananda's 'secret'. He systematically sought to deny the place of Kali worship in any version of Hinduism. The masses had to be taught only Vedanta. Kali worship was his special prerogative. He called it 'my special fad'.[15] Hinduism had to be cleansed of all tantric, puranic and bhakti influences and recreated upon the solid foundation of Vedanta. If this meant a denial or a reinterpretation of the central tenets of Sri Ramakrishna, Vivekananda was more than ready to do so. Scriptures and teachers were nothing more than facilitators. Even without them, one could still realize the truth 'within'.[16] It would be much later that Vivekananda would propose his ideas of Practical Vedanta, with its implications for Hindu society.

II

A single event helped create a timeless mystique around Swami Vivekananda. This was his address at the World's Parliament of Religions in Chicago on 11 September 1893. Even to this day, his address is seen by many as a turning point in Hindu reassertion and revival. Contemporary votaries of 'soft' Hindutva, from A.B. Bardhan to A.B. Vajpayee, swear by the spirit of his message in Chicago. Liberals, leftists and communalists are joined together in appropriating the legacy of Vivekananda as put forth in this address. What was so special about this piece of oration delivered to the 'Sisters and Brothers of America'?[17] In a masterful way, Vivekananda addressed three major concerns of nineteenth-century India: Hindu identity, Hindu nationalism and an equal 'dialogue' between Hinduism and other faiths.

At the outset, Vivekananda categorically asserted the pre-eminence of Hinduism by calling it 'the mother of religions'.[18] This claim of superiority rested on the fact that Hinduism was that religion which had *taught*, and continued to teach, the world both tolerance and universal acceptance. Not only did Hinduism believe in tolerance but it also accepted all religions as true. It had never persecuted, either with sword or pen, and in fact had given shelter to persecuted sects. Its message was the surest antidote to sectarianism, bigotry and fanaticism. In one deft stroke, Vivekananda defined Hinduism's equation with all other faiths: They were mere children in relation to the 'mother of religions', and also were participants in an eternal seminar, where the 'tutor' was Hinduism and the 'tutees' were all other faiths.

The Swami spoke again at the Parliament of Religions on 19 September 1893.[19] He restated his position on Hinduism being a tolerant and all-embracing faith. It was a superior faith because it did not believe in the inevitability of a dreadful combination of unforgiving laws and was not inextricably bound to an endless cycle of cause and effect. The only condition that Hinduism placed on the individual was purity. God's mercy visited only the pure, and it did so even in this life. The moment one approaches God with a pure heart, all causation and all 'crookedness of the heart'[20] cease to matter. Hinduism was, therefore, devoid of the compulsion to believe in any dogma or doctrine. Its core lay in 'being and becoming'.[21] What does this being and becoming comprise? In moving from lower truth to higher truth, and not from error to truth as suggested by other faiths. This flight from lower truth or apara vidya to higher truth or para vidya remained a constant theme in Vivekananda's life and thought.

Just as an individual travelled from lower truth to higher truth, so was the case with religions. Hinduism accepted all religions, from the lowest form of fetishism to the highest form of absolutism, as 'attempts of the human soul to grasp and realize the Infinite'.[22] The triumph of Hinduism was in recognizing that the Absolute could be realized only through the help of the relative, manifest in images, idols, crosses and crescents. These were 'so many pegs to hang the spiritual ideas on'.[23] All recognized faiths went through this evolution. They began with the idea of the universe being created by God. This included the idea of inspiration and revealed books. Soon emerged the idea of a soul as distinct from the body, but as an entity that was encapsulated within the body. This, according to Vivekananda, is the most primitive form of religion.[24]

Hinduism gave up this primitive idea very early. It discovered a grand explanation for the unity and oneness of all religions. This was encapsulated in the proposition *Ekam Sat Vipraa Bahudhaa Vadanti*—That which exists is One; sages call It by various names.[25] This allowed theists, atheists, monists, dualists, materialists, monotheists, Buddhists, Jains, Muslims and Christians to preach in

India without being persecuted. This sense of tolerance and unity, affirmed Vivekananda, had 'entered into the blood of the nation'.[26]

Having dwelt on the theme of tolerance, Vivekananda now started taking other faiths to task. All other religions, asserted Vivekananda, suffer from the fatal flaws of faith in a Personal God, sectarianism, bigotry and fanaticism. This assertion flowed from his formal definition of religion:

> Religion is not talk, or doctrines or theories, nor is it sectarianism. Religion cannot live in sects and societies. It is the relation between the soul and God; how can it be made into a society?[27]

The first stumbling block in approximating to this idea, therefore, was the notion of a Personal God. This idea carried with itself the notion of imparting certain attributes to God. There was a constant process of inclusion and exclusion inherent in this—God is all merciful, all good, but he is also not evil. As a viable notion of God, it could never lend itself to a satisfactory generalization.[28] The Impersonal God of Hinduism was not a relative God. It was not a creation of our own limited contexts. No sensible religion, Vivekananda felt, would, therefore, permit prayers to God; asking God to bring rain, to give us our daily bread and so on smacked of materialism. For these one could pray to the gods who were usually saints or incarnations of God. But to pray to God himself was sheer blasphemy. We must go to God for higher things.[29]

Further, all religions, with the sole exception of Hinduism, depended on the historical veracity of their founders or prophets. This invariably led to conflict.[30] Tearing apart the prophetic tradition, he debunks the very motives of all prophets (with the exception of the Buddha). All prophets were moved by external motives to expect reward from the outside, meaning the material world. Their actions were not unselfish. Their language may have been highly evolved but their intentions were highly suspect.[31]

Having said this, Vivekananda went on to reject the idea that prophets of other religions were even spiritually evolved. An elevated soul usually went beyond reason and also transcended his ordinary human nature. There were individuals, however, who merely stumbled upon this state.

> The Yogi says there is a great danger in stumbling upon this state. In a good many cases there is the danger of the brain being deranged, and, as a rule, you will find that all those men, however great they were, who had stumbled upon this superconscious state without understanding it, groped in the dark, and generally had along with their knowledge, some quaint superstitions. They opened themselves to hallucinations.[32]

At this juncture, Vivekananda begins to give concrete examples from other religions and their particular characteristics.

The most obvious example, according to Vivekananda, of this state of hallucination mentioned above was that of Prophet Muhammad.

> Mohammed claimed that the Angel Gabriel came to him in a cave one day and took him on the heavenly

> horse, Harak, and he visited the heavens. But with all that, Mohammed spoke some wonderful truths. If you read the Koran, you will find the most wonderful truths mixed with superstitions. How will you explain it? That man was inspired, no doubt, but that inspiration was, as it were, stumbled upon. He was not a trained Yogi, and did not know the reason of what he was doing. Think of the good Mohammed did to the world, and think of the great evil that has been done through his fanaticism![33]

In short, Islam and the Prophet propagated some wonderful truths but, like most monotheistic sects, brought about a great deal of cruelty and persecution.[34]

Vivekananda was often torn between the idealism in Islam and its historical role in India in particular, and the world in general. He felt that people often found it difficult to comprehend the religious fervour that impelled Prophet Muhammad. The Prophet's grovelling in the dust and writhing in agony were extreme emotions that had often been termed by people as an epileptic condition.[35] On 25 March 1900, Vivekananda delivered a lecture in San Francisco on Prophet Muhammad.[36] It is a crucial text in understanding Vivekananda's view of Islam, the legitimacy of his claim of Hinduism as a tolerant and universal faith, as well as his delineation of the ingredients that have gone into influencing political Hindutva's perception of Islam.

Vivekananda began his lecture on Prophet Muhammad with a tribute to Lord Krishna. It was Krishna, he asserted, whose message harmonized the teachings of the Buddha, Christ and Muhammad. Krishna antedated all other prophets. All other prophets had an 'idea' but took this 'idea' to an extreme. Only Krishna brought about a perfect harmony between all these ideas. Having made these opening remarks, Vivekananda went on to introduce the Prophet:

> Mohammed [as] a young man ... did not [seem to] care much for religion. He was inclined to make money. He was considered a nice young man and very handsome. There was a rich widow. She fell in love with this young man, and they married. When Mohammed had become emperor over the larger part of the world, the Roman and Persian empires were all under his feet, and he had a number of wives. When one day he was asked which wife he liked best, he pointed to his first wife: 'Because she believed [in] me first.'[37]

Vivekananda returns to this theme of Muhammad marrying a number of wives again in the course of the lecture. Great men may marry two hundred wives, he states. Their characters are mysterious. We must not judge them.[38]

Turning to religion, Vivekananda argued that Muhammad struck against sin, idolatry, mock worship, superstitions prevalent during his time. He prayed and had the vision of Gabriel who told him he was the messenger of truth. The Prophet saw Christians preaching politics instead of the message of Jesus and the Persians preaching dualism. He, therefore, declared that there was one God who was the Lord of all that existed. Between this God and other gods, there was no comparison. A faith emerged out of this. What was it? Viveknnanda describes it as follows:

> God is God. There is no philosophy, no complicated code of ethics. 'Our God is one without a second, and Mohammed is the Prophet.' ... Mohammed began to preach it in the streets of Mecca ... They began to persecute him, and he fled into the city of [Medina]. He began to fight, and the whole race became united. [Mohammedanism] deluged the world in the name of the Lord. The tremendous conquering power![39]

Islam's message was for the masses. Vivekananda perceived equality as the central message of Islam. There was to be no distinction of race or colour. It was a practical message, it asked its followers to believe in one God and ask no questions. Vivekananda ended his lecture calling the Prophet a great messenger of light and a great teacher.

The above lecture gives only a partial picture of Vivekananda's views on Islam. One could argue that, delivered in 1900, it does represent Vivekananda's mature views. But there were other occasions when his comments did not betray such admirable moderation. For instance, Islam came in for harsh comments from him when he discussed the need to make religion subservient to reason, and held that reason was the only way to arrive at a true judgement of the relative merits and demerits of religions.

> It is clearly stated in the Koran, 'Kill the infidels if they do not become Mohemmedans. They must be put to fire and sword.' Now if we tell a Mohemmedan that this is wrong, he will naturally ask: 'How do you know that? How do you know it is not good? My book says it is.' If you say your book is older, there will come

> the Buddhist, and say, my book is much older still ... Therefore referring to books will not do.[40]

Islam, for Vivekananda, was built upon a degree of narrow-mindedness and claims of knowing God's will. This bred a great degree of arrogance among its followers. The march of Islam was on the strength of sword in one hand and the Qur'an in the other hand.[41] Nothing could resist this combination for hundreds of years.

Vivekananda felt that Islam was too 'bound to itself'.[42] This produced its own dynamic of selfishness and immorality. In turn, this combination produces unprecedented wickedness and cruelty:

> There has not been a religion that has clung to this dualism more than that founded by the Prophet of Arabia, and there has not been a religion which has shed so much blood and been so cruel to other men. In the Koran there is the doctrine that a man who does not believe these teachings should be killed; it is a mercy to kill him! And the surest way to get to heaven, where there are beautiful houris, and all sorts of sense enjoyments, is by killing these unbelievers. Think of the bloodshed there has been in consequence of such beliefs![43]

There were, however, men in Islam who exhibited the 'touch of the Divine',[44] and this led to a broadening of the mind and heart. In the absence of such men, and bereft of the 'touch of the Divine', Muslims were sectarian to the core.

> Now, the Mohammedans are the crudest in this respect, and the most sectarian. Their watchword is, 'There is one God and Mahomed is His Prophet.' Everything beyond that, not only is bad, but must be destroyed forthwith; at a moment's notice, every man or woman who does not belong to this worship must be immediately broken; every book that teaches anything else must be burnt. From the Pacific to the Atlantic, for five hundred years blood ran all over the world. That is Mohammedanism![45]

Despite the onward march of Islam, this religion of sword and fire, the 'core' or the 'centre' of Indian nationality was untouched. This 'core', for Vivekananda, was religion—more specifically, Hindu religion. Barbarian conquests could not shake or destroy this core. This is how Vivekananda described the advent of Islam in India:

> Wave after wave of barbarian conquest has rolled over this devoted land of ours. 'Allah Ho Akbar!' has rent the skies for hundreds of years, and no Hindu knew what moment would be his last.[46]

Vivekananda pointed out that the Muslims hated Hindus more than the Jews and the Christians. For them Hindus were hated kafirs, idolators, and deserved to be butchered. Their ire was directed specially against the priestly caste in India, for they were the spiritual guides of the kafirs. If a Muslim ruler was extremely devout, the end result would be a 'great Yajna, by way of Kafir-slaughter!'[47] India stopped progressing during the Muslim rule in India. The question of progress did not arise, says Vivekananda, because all the energies of the Hindus were directed towards self-preservation.[48]

Even the Bhakti movement in northern India was an attempt to restrain the Hindu masses converting to Islam. Vivekananda acknowledges that Islam did contribute to bringing about social and spiritual equality for the masses, but it also sapped the energies of the likes of Ramananda, Kabir, Dadu, Chaitanya and Nanak; they were solely preoccupied with checking the rapid conquest of Islam among the masses. As a result they failed to give birth to new ideas and hopes.[49]

As seen in the following sections, Vivekananda as Vedantin and reformer of Hinduism would have much to say about the merits and the goodness inherent in Islam. But as a religious preacher, he was committed to showing Hinduism in a superior light. Ironically, in order to dramatize the centrality of tolerance in Hinduism—a core theme of his Chicago address—Vivekananda became a prisoner of history. He had to illustrate that Hinduism had never persecuted, never conquered, never resorted to sword and fire. In doing so, he chose unfortunate examples. The question was not one of historical authenticity. It was one of transcending the limiting role of history in order to fabricate a truly universal faith.

Islam alone was not the target of Vivekananda's indictment. In his evolutionary schema of religions, only Hinduism had managed to reach maturity in thought. After all, it was, in his own words, the mother of religions. It had also assumed the role of a teacher to other religions. Other religions, therefore, had to be imparted instruction, and the errant among them had to be suitably chastised.

Christianity was among such 'pupils', though it fared marginally better than Islam in Vivekananda's eyes.

Vivekananda saw Christianity in India largely through the prism of the activities of Christian missionaries in India. Though he saw Jesus as a pure spirit, he felt Jesus' message had been perverted by his followers. At one point Vivekananda went to the extent of saying that there was little difference between 'the pure religion of Christ and that of the Vedanta'.[50] But he went on to suggest that crudeness had soon crept into the original message of Jesus, and Christianity was reduced to something 'not much better than the religion of the Prophet of Arabia.'[51]

> It was crudeness indeed,—this flight for the little self, this clinging on to the 'I', not only in this life, but also in the desire for its continuance even after death.[52]

This preoccupation with the 'I' was in direct contrast with the pure spirit of Jesus which was inward-looking and aspired to reach beyond the phenomenal world. In direct contradiction to the spirit of Jesus, Christianity, like all millennial sects, promised that God would come to rule the universe and bring about perfect harmony and equality. This promise of equality made Christianity fascinating to the Greek and Roman slaves who were the first converts to the faith—a barely concealed allusion to the conversion of lower-caste Hindus.

Christians in India were prone to be luxury-loving, insolent, despotic and intolerant. They hurled abuses at Indian customs and traditions. Vivekananda felt that the true message of Jesus was one of renunciation and poverty.

Christianity had clearly deviated from this goal. Yet as an Oriental, said Vivekananda, the only way to worship Jesus was to 'worship him as God and nothing else'.[53]

To reiterate, for Vivekananda Hinduism was the mother of all religions. It could also teach other faiths tolerance and universal brotherhood. Unlike most other faiths, Hinduism never persecuted and never conquered. In the evolutionary schema of religions, it had already perfected itself. Most other faiths were given to dogmatism, bigotry, violence and fanaticism. Only Hinduism believed that despite their failings, all religions were but many ways to reach the ultimate truth.

It was against this background that Vivekananda proposed his theory of Hindu tolerance. It fits in uneasily with his earlier typology of all other religions, except Hinduism, as participants in a process of eventual perfection. The idea of Hindu superiority was also implicit in Vivekananda's attempt to propose such a theory. The first rhetorical step in positing a theory of Hindu tolerance was, therefore, to refrain from judging other faiths.[54] According to Vivekananda, we tend to reduce everyone else to the limits of our own mental universe and begin privileging our own ethics, morality, sense of duty and even our sense of utility. All religious conflicts arose from this propensity to judge others. If we indeed must judge at all, argued Vivekananda, it must be 'according to his own ideal, and not by that of anyone else'.[55] It was important, therefore, to learn to look at the duty of others through their own eyes and never judge the customs and observances of others through the prism of our own standards. This was the very foundation upon which the edifice of tolerance stood. Hinduism, says Vivekananda, was built on a similar foundation, or to put it more correctly, was the foundation itself.

All religions, asserts Vivekananda, are at different stages of a journey. The aim of each one of them is 'the perfect conception of the Vedas'.[56] Therefore, every idea of God and every religion was true. This followed from the premise that the Vedas 'contain the essence of all religions',[57] though the Vedas did not alone contain the truth. Vivekananda did not always remember to add this last caveat. Hinduism, therefore, not only *tolerated* but also *accepted* every religion. Vivekananda began with the thesis of toleration, moved on quickly to add another dimension, namely, acceptance, and then, with equal alacrity, subverted the 'tolerance' argument in favour of fellow feeling. Tolerance was condescending, patronizing, and a niggardly expression of goodwill.

> Toleration means that I think you are wrong and I am just allowing you to live. Is it not blasphemy to think that you and I are allowing others to live?[58]

Vivekananda, then, proceeded to describe this intense identification with other faiths:

> I accept all religions that were in the past, and worship God with everyone of them, in whatever form they worship Him.[59]

What, then, was required is that humans ought to become many-sided. Vivekananda maintained that we must become Protean in character, so that we may not only tolerate, but also 'do what is much more difficult, to sympathise, to enter into another's path, and feel *with him* in his aspirations and seeking after God.'[60] To deride the God of another religion was to deride your own God.

Hinduism was the repository of such tolerance, acceptance and sympathy. The first step towards this admirable goal was to see God in every person. The next step was to feel that oneness. Once this was accomplished, we would be able to transcend our limited phenomenal world and become immortal.[61] Vedanta allowed this sense of oneness while promoting an infinite variety and variation in religious thought.

Therefore, the Vedanta lays down that each man should be treated not as what he manifests, but as what he stands for. Each human being stands for the divine, and, therefore, every teacher should be helpful, not by condemning man, but by helping him to call forth the divinity that is within him.[62]

Vedanta, then, provided the surest and the most solid basis for universal ethics. This did not, however, hold true in the case of other religions. Note in the ensuing quotes, firstly, a thinly veiled denunciation of Christian ethics, and secondly, Vivekananda's belief that there was a natural, evolutionary hierarchy among religions.

> Though all religions have taught ethical precepts, such as, 'Do not kill, do not injure; love your neighbour as yourself,' etc., yet none of these has given the reason. Why should I not injure my neighbour? To this question there was no satisfactory answer forthcoming, until it was evolved by the metaphysical speculations

> of the Hindus who could not rest satisfied with mere dogmas.[63]

The Hindus had rejected dogmas masquerading as ethics. What was the alternative proposed by the metaphysical speculations of the Hindus?

> So the Hindus say that this Atman is absolute and all pervading, therefore infinite. There cannot be two infinites, for they would limit each other and would become finite. Also each individual soul is a part and parcel of that Universal Soul, which is infinite. Therefore, in injuring his neighbour, the individual actually injures himself. This is the basic metaphysical truth underlying all ethical codes.[64]

Hinduism, therefore, embodied the perfection of the religious idea itself. In this sense, it encapsulated within itself the truths of all religions:

> It is the recognition of this truth, which has enabled the Hindus to perceive the universal truth of all religions from the *lowest to the highest;* it has made of them the only people who never had religious persecutions. The shrine of a Mohammedan saint, which is at the present day neglected and forgotten by Mohammedans, is worshipped by Hindus! Many instances may be quoted, illustrating the same spirit of tolerance.[65]

And, therefore the only way to reach this state of tolerance and universal brotherhood was to accept the supremacy of the Vedas. Here, Vivekananda's argument comes full circle:

> And as the Vedas are the Scriptures which teach this real absolute God, of which all *other ideas of God are but minimized and limited versions* ... and as all other religions represent one or the other of these stages in an unprogressive and crystallized form, all other religions of the world are included in the nameless, limitless, eternal Vedic religion.[66]

The lofty flights of Advaita were, therefore, of little help to Vivekananda in forgetting the past. History cast its shadow on the whole idea of oneness and fellow feeling. Hindus must build churches and mosques in India, asserted Vivekananda, despite the hatred, brutality, cruelty, tyranny and the vile language of the Muslims and Christians. He hoped that such proactive love would ultimately win.[67] Yet, Vivekananda could never take that all-important leap into rejecting sweeping racial and religious stereotypes. When he says Muslims, he meant *all* Muslims, and so with Christians. (The subtlety of the idea of rejecting English rule but not the English had to wait for more than a decade for Gandhi to formulate it.)

The idea of Hinduism as a tolerant, all-embracing and non-antagonistic faith was extremely crucial to Vivekanandn's project of restating Hinduism for the world at large. He presented it as an ideal. Again and again, Vivekananda was confronted with the question, how long should one tolerate? His answer on such occasions was clear: As long as one is tolerated:

> But when we see men coming and saying, 'this is the only way,' and trying to force it on us in India, we have a word to say; we laugh at them. For such people

> who want to destroy their brothers because they seem to follow a different path towards God,—for them to talk of love is absurd.[68]

The ideal of tolerance and sympathy, therefore, could be extremely tenuous and fragile. It was not tenable for all times and all contexts. Reality often intruded into the idyllic world of such noble ideas.

Vivekananda derived the idea of a common universal faith from Sri Ramakrishna. In a speech delivered in New York, and subsequently published under the title, 'My Master',[69] Vivekananda speaks of Sri Ramakrishna's attempt to know the truth of all other faiths. The passage reproduced below illustrates why Vivekananda's own attempt at arriving at a viable notion of Hinduism as a tolerant faith was a 'failure'.

> The next desire that seized the soul of this man was to know the truth about the various religions. Upto that time he had not known any religion but his own. He wanted to understand what other religions were like. So he sought teachers of other religions. By teachers you must always remember what we mean in India—not a book-worm, but a man of realization, one who knows truth at first-hand and not through an intermediary. He found a Mahomedan saint and went to live with him; he underwent the disciplines prescribed by him, and to his astonishment found that when faithfully carried out, these devotional methods led him to the same goal he had already attained. He gathered similar experience from following the true religion of Jesus the Christ. He went to all the sects he could find, and whatever he took

> up he went into with his whole heart. He did exactly as he was told, and in every instance he arrived at the same result. Thus from actual experience, he came to know that the goal of every religion is the same, that each is trying to teach the same thing, the difference being largely in method, and still more in language. At the core, all sects and all religions have the same aim, and they were only quarrelling for their own selfish purposes; they were not anxious about the truth, but about 'my name' and 'your name'.[70]

Vivekananda did not experience this oneness of faiths like Sri Ramakrishna. His attempt remained confined to the intellectual plane and lacked the intensity of living another man's faith with one's 'whole heart'. Between Sri Ramakrishna and Swami Vivekananda, the disparity in method to arrive at the same conclusion made all the difference. Like Jesus, Sri Ramakrishna was after all the pure sort, unencumbered by history or context, but immensely rich in experience. Vivekananda was like Paul, the thundering sort, who had to spread the light quickly and effectively. He understood well that religion was not an intellectual activity but an act of realization. But he was often impatient. Hinduism as a tolerant and all-embracing faith remained for him an aspiration, never an experience.

III

Vivekananda reached Colombo on 15 January 1897 after spending nearly four years in the West. On 16 January, he gave a public lecture at the Floral Hall in Colombo. In his address, he pronounced India to be the punya bhoomi,[71] the land where all souls aspiring towards a spiritual quest must come to attain their last home. This was the land, he felt, where all souls must invariably come to account for their karma. India was punya bhoomi because humanity here had attained the highest summits in gentleness, generosity, purity, calmness, introspection and spirituality.[72] The world owed much to the 'mild Hindu',[73] who exemplified these wonderful qualities. Vivekananda's formulation of the notion would predate V.D. Savarkar's by several decades.

As would Savarkar, Vivekananda formulated his idea of India in terms of an eternal civilization that owed its origins to the Aryans. India was eternal because the same laws and customs as in the days of Manu had continued, though with adjustments and modifications. Misfortunes or adversities did not affect the edifice of Eternal India. This India was also essentially Aryan. The imperative of defining a nation in terms of homogeneous racial types led Vivekananda to assert emphatically that the 'whole of India is Aryan, nothing else'.[74]

Not that Vivekananda was unaware of the great confluence of races in India and their assimilation in the national fabric over thousands of years. He asserted that this assimilation was accomplished through gentle and non-coercive means. While he admitted that races are invariably mixed, and that the idea of a 'pure' race was a logical infelicity, he also said that despite this fusion of racial types, India had found a common racial background in the form of the Aryas.[75] The epithet 'Arya', according to Vivekananda, applied to both the 'great races' in India, the Sanskrit-speaking and the Tamil-speaking Hindus.

Otherwise, the Aryan and Dravidian divide was one of language, not blood.[76]

The 'madness of confluence of races'[77] in India could have created chaos and anarchy. But this was not the case in India. A superior culture brought about a semblance of order in what could have been the very reason of India's undoing. This superior culture was the gift of the Aryans and their caste system. Within the caste system, it was the role of the Brahmins that heralded this superior culture:

> It [the caste system] put, theoretically at least, the whole of India under the guidance—not of wealth, nor of the sword—but of intellect—intellect chastened and controlled by spirituality. The leading caste in India is the highest of the Aryans—the Brahmans.[78]

Apologists of Vivekananda have often seen him as a great opponent of caste. This is only partially true. While he was contemptuous of untouchability and did not favour an excessive preoccupation with ritual purity, the caste ideal was central to his plan for the regeneration of India. His statements like, 'we are just "Don't-touchists." Our religion is in the kitchen. Our God is the cooking-pot, and our religion is "Don't touch me, I am holy",'[79] are often read as examples of his anti-caste stance. The evidence indicates otherwise.

According to Vivekananda, the Indian caste system was one of the 'greatest social institutions the Lord gave to man'.[80] It is true that this great social institution had often been thwarted from performing its legitimate functions by foreign invaders as well as by ignorant and arrogant Brahmins, but despite these limitations it had 'already worked wonders for the land of Bharata'.[81] It was this institution that was destined to lead Indians towards achieving their goals and aspirations. Going a step further, Vivekananda attributed the downfall of India to a thoughtless rejection of caste. The original idea of caste was premised on the notion of diversity. Creation stopped when there was no diversity—'unity is before creation, diversity is creation'—this is how Vivekananda formulated the central axiom about caste.[82] The original idea of caste, he said, was to give an individual the freedom to express his nature, his prakriti. It was not based on custom, privilege or inheritance. This crystallization of caste on the basis of privilege and heredity was a modern-day distortion. His exhortation to his countrymen was to regain the lost glory of this unique institution:

> Therefore what I have to tell you, my countrymen, is this:—That India fell because you prevented and abolished caste ... Let Jati have its sway; break down every barrier in the way of caste and we shall rise.[83]

Caste, therefore, was a natural order, a natural way of ordering life. The only thing to guard against was the idea of privilege. Higher castes must not trample upon the heads of the lower castes. In modern India, caste had become a 'crystallized social institution', confined to wilfulness of the priestly caste. Caste had assumed a rigidity that went against its original mandate of fostering people's social individuality. It was now 'filling the atmosphere of India with its stench'.[84] The way out of this was to go back to the first principles of caste as a diversity-enhancing institution.

The task before India, asserted Vivekananda, was to redivide the entire Hindu population on the basis of the four main castes, the Brahmins, Kshatriyas, Vaishyas and Sudras.[85] All subdivisions among these main groupings will have to be abolished. There will be a single Brahmin caste, and so will be the case with the other three castes. An approximation to the Vedic ideal will, therefore, be achieved.

In doing so, the need was to raise the lower caste to the level of the higher caste rather than bringing down the higher caste. Vivekananda envisaged a new Satyayuga dawning on India where the Brahmin would have pride of place. Indeed, the Brahmin was the ideal India had to emulate:

> The Brahmanhood is the ideal of humanity in India, as wonderfully put forward by Sankaracharya at the beginning of his commentary on the Gita, where he speaks about the reason for Krishna's coming as a preacher for the preservation of Brahmanhood, of Brahmanness.[86]

The ideal, therefore, was to raise the Chandala, the lowest of the Sudras, to the level of the Brahmin. Indeed, it was the duty of the Brahmin to work for the salvation of the rest of mankind. As long as the Brahmin did that, he was worthy of being called a Brahmin. The Brahmin had been a trustee of the 'accumulated culture of ages'.[87] It was now his duty to spread that culture among all people.

Vivekananda had little sympathy, however, with the Brahmins of his day. He blamed them for sucking the blood of millions of poor people without the slightest trace of effort on their part to ameliorate the condition of the poor and the destitute.[88] He went as far as likening the Brahmins of Kaliyuga to rakshasas.[89] Despite these disclaimers, he was firm in the belief that the Brahmin was the ideal of humanity for India. Though Vivekananda was eloquent about the need to emancipate the lot of the 'proletariat', he had an innate distrust of what he called the 'multitude'.[90] The cultured among a community were the real custodians of religion and philosophy, he felt, and the moment these fell into the hands of the multitude, degradation was the end result.

To the lower castes, Vivekananda had an unambiguous message: Learn Sanskrit. He felt that along with the language of the people, Sanskrit was a must. Sanskrit, he argued, gave 'a prestige and a power and a strength to the race'.[91] All great seers and prophets made one great mistake: They did not encourage dissemination of Sanskrit among the masses and the lower classes. Ramanuja, Chaitanya, Kabir and the Buddha were all guilty of this false step.

> The only safety, I tell you men who belong to the lower castes, the only way to raise your condition is to study Sanskrit, and this fighting and writing and frothing against the higher castes is in vain, it does no good, and it creates fight and quarrel, and this race, unfortunately already divided, is going to be divided more and more.[92]

India's future as envisaged by Vivekananda would consist, then, of only three castes, the Brahmins, Kshatriyas and Vaishyas. The Sudras would graduate to the upper castes. But how was this to happen?

Vivekananda was conscious of the fact that several Hindu scriptures left the Sudras out of the 'Aryan' category. In response to this exclusion, he held that Sudras were and are 'only the waiting Aryas,—Aryas in novitiate'.[93] They would, he hoped, lift themselves to the level of the Brahmins, and the Brahmins would give them a helping hand in this process. Modern machinery would also assist in their emancipation. Vivekananda envisaged a future India where the Sudra caste would be eliminated altogether because machines would do their work.[94] Elsewhere, Vivekananda felt that the current epoch, Kaliyuga, belonged to the Sudra. The first three castes had had their day. The onward march of the Sudra was inevitable and irresistible.[95] The advantages of a Sudra-centric epoch would be the widespread distribution of physical comforts and spread of ordinary education. Its disadvantages would, perhaps, be the lowering of culture; society would produce fewer and fewer geniuses.[96]

India was the punya bhoomi. It was Eternal India. Eternal India was Hindu. It was Hindu and Aryan. Aryans made India eternal and holy. But there was a confluence of races in this land. This could have generated chaos and anarchy, but this potential problem was admirably dealt with by a superior culture. This culture was the direct outcome of the primacy of the intellect of the Brahmins. Also, the caste system brought about a semblance of order in what would otherwise be chaos and anarchy amidst such diversity of races. Having argued thus, Vivekananda had to now account for the enslavement of India. In his analysis, Vivekananda cited rejection of caste as one of the reasons for India's status as a slave nation. But this was surely not the only reason.

Vivekananda believed that India's woes were the result of a rupture with its past.[97] India to him was always the Hindu nation. The Hindus had stopped looking into their past, and as a consequence, were pushed into a state of stupor. He was hopeful that they had begun, once again, to delve into their past and this was the first step towards creation of a glorious future. A dislocation with the past had made India degenerate. Vivekananda systematically listed the consequences of this break from the Hindu past:

- People are guided like lifeless machines;
- There is no mental activity, no unfoldment of the heart, no vibration of life, no flux of hope;
- There is no strong stimulation of the will, no experience of keen pleasure, nor the contract of intense sorrow;
- There is no stir of inventive genius, no desire for novelty, no appreciation of new things.[98]

Indian society was constituted by men who were nothing more than 'lumps of clay'.[99] They were lifeless automatons and were similar to 'heaped up pebbles'.[100] The Hindu nation could have been the greatest nation on earth and become the eternal fountainhead of learning. Instead, slavery for hundreds of years had reduced it to being a 'mine of stupidity'.[101]

> Clouds never pass away from this mind, the radiant picture of the morning sun never charms the heart. It never even occurs to this mind if there is any better state than this; where it does, it cannot convince; in the

event of conviction, effort is lacking; and even where there is effort, lack of enthusiasm kills it.[102]

The Hindu capacity for logical thought and metaphysics was also its undoing. This great mental power got exaggerated and led to denial of action in favour of renunciation and introspection.[103] It is action with desire, insisted Vivekananda, which must eventually lead to action without desire. Renunciation of desire without the existence of desire in the first instance was absurd. The consequence of this attitude was a disastrous neglect of material civilization by the Hindus.[104] Because of this neglect the Muslims conquered them. In a bitter aside, Vivekananda quipped that the Muslims even taught the Hindus to wear tailor-made clothes.[105]

Neglect of material civilization led to poverty, which, in turn, led to dehumanization.[106] Slavery was the direct consequence of dehumanization. Indians had been reduced to 'three hundred millions of earth-worms crawling'[107] on the soil of India and trying to oppress each other. Vivekananda laid the blame for the degradation of India squarely on its inability to feed itself. This created a culture of dependence. It led to conversions among the Hindu poor to Islam and Christianity. The wall of custom added to this oppression. The stranglehold of shastric injunctions might make men do a few things well, but ultimately stifled free will and initiative.[108] Whatever may have been the original motive of these customs, they had induced people to hate each other.[109] India's doom was inevitable, Vivekananda asserted, the day the word 'mlechchha' was coined. From that moment onwards,

Indians stopped communion with others and became insular.[110]

Another factor that compounded India's wretchedness was the lack of a notion of self-government.[111] India had been ruled by a succession of godlike kings, who had the sole responsibility of protecting and providing for the people. The common people did not exert themselves for the common good or for even self-preservation, and, consequently, lost all their vitality and strength. In other words, the nation had lost its individuality.[112] It had been trampled underfoot by Hindus, Muslims and Christians alike. This was the cause of India's degeneration.

The first step Vivekananda suggested by way of India's emancipation was overcoming physical weakness. All else, including religion, could wait before accomplishing this all-important task. The young, he felt, would be 'nearer to Heaven through football than through the study of the Gita'.[113] The satva guna, the constellation of sublime virtues, invariably led to non-action, laziness and lack of originality. It was imperative for India to pass through a stage where rajas—strength, valour and action—was privileged.

> You will understand Gita better with your biceps, your muscles, a little stronger. You will understand the mighty genius and the mighty strength of Krishna better with a little strong blood in you. You will understand the Upanishads better and the glory of the Atman, when your body stands firm upon your feet, and you feel yourself as men.[114]

In a letter written in 1895,[115] Vivekananda promises to make men out of the people of India. India was, he felt, inhabited only by women, eunuchs and imbeciles. It was his task to instill manhood in them.

Bhakti, especially the form espoused by Chaitanya, was one of the reasons for loss of manliness in India. Chaitanya's Radha-prema suggested that the devotee ought to exhibit the same measure of love for Krishna as Radha had done.

> Look at this nation and see what has been the outcome of such attempt. Through the preaching of that love broadcast, the whole nation has become effeminate—a race of women! The whole of Orissa has been turned into a land of cowards; and Bengal, running after that Radha-prema, these past four hundred years, has almost lost all sense of manliness! The people are very good only at crying and weeping; that has become their national trait. Look at their literature, the sure index of a nation's thoughts and ideas. Why, the refrain of the Bengali literature for four hundred years is strung to that same tune of moaning and crying. It has failed to give birth to any poetry which breathes a true heroic spirit![116]

Vivekananda was clear that the aspect or form of Sri Krishna in Vrindavan, where he is shown to be playing the flute and engaging with the gopis in raas-lila, had to be underplayed.[117] Rather, the Krishna of the Mahabharata, 'roaring the Gita out, with the voice of a lion',[118] was the model to be emulated. The other role models recommended by Vivekananda for inculcating manliness were Sri Ramachandra, Hanuman and Sri Ramakrishna. He insisted that the worship of Sri Ramachandra and Hanuman be introduced in every home in India. Only this could pave the way for the welfare of the country.

While Vivekananda detested the 'moaning and crying' aspect of women, he was a votary of the worship of Shakti, the divine manifestation of God as power.[119] Only then, observed Vivekananda, would people feel rajas or valour thrilling through their veins. Unlike many contemporaries of his, Vivekananda did not attribute manliness to the Kshatriyas alone.[120] He wanted 'muscles of iron and nerves of steel', but this model of manhood was to be concocted through a combination of the valour of the Kshatriya, Kshatra-virya, and power of the intellect of the Brahmin, Brahma-teja.[121] He also greatly admired the Yavanas (Greek) for their energy, love of independence, spirit of self-reliance, action, unity of purpose and thirst for improvement.[122] As the 'forefathers' of modern Europe and America, they were worthy of emulation too. They represented rajas or valour at its best.

Vivekananda was clearly no pacifist. Recent attempts to portray Vivekananda's thought as an early intimation of Gandhi's philosophy of non-violence clearly miss the mark. Unambiguously stated, Vivekananda's project of revitalizing Hinduism and the Hindu nation had a legitimate place for the 'eye for an eye, tooth for a tooth' principle. He often went beyond the conventionally prescribed dose of retaliation. He arrived at this position through a very interesting trajectory.

Vivekananda firmly believed in varnadharma, the duties prescribed by one's caste, and ashramadharma, the duties prescribed during various stages in an individual's life. He felt that the pursuit of moksha, ending the cycles of birth and death through renunciation, had been given undue importance by some, and misunderstood entirely by others. Humans must pursue artha, wealth, dharma, duties of one's station, kama, pleasure, and moksha, renunciation, according to the terms set by varnadharma and ashramadharma. While others seemed to have privileged moksha over other pursuits, Vivekananda privileged dharma over all other human goals.

> The Hindu scriptures say, 'No doubt, Moksha is far superior to Dharma; but Dharma should be finished first of all.' The Bauddhas were confounded just there and brought about all sorts of mischief. Non-injury is right. 'Resist not evil' is a great thing—these are indeed grand principles; but the Shastras say, 'Thou art a householder; if anyone smites thee on the cheek, and thou dost not return him an eye for an eye, a tooth for a tooth, thou wilt verily be a sinner.' Manu says, 'When one has come to kill you, there is no sin in killing him, even though he is a Brahmana.' (Manu, VIII. 350) This is very true, and this is a thing which should not be forgotten.[123]

Clearly, there is a confounding of two very different ideas here. The ethics of 'eye for an eye' and 'tooth for a tooth' generates an unending spiral of revenge and retaliatory violence. Not striking out when one's life is in danger is not pacifism but cowardice. Even committed pacifists would accept retaliation as a legitimate form of self-defence. Vivekananda never did make this distinction. For him, retaliation deserved counter-retaliation. He literally went ten steps further.

> If one gets one blow, one must return ten with redoubled fury ... then only one is a man ... the coward is an object to be pitied.[124]

Further, he goes on to define the true Dharmika as one who follows the fourfold political maxims of conciliation, bribery, sowing dissensions and open war to win over an adversary.[125] He blames the Jains and the Buddhists for transforming the Hindus into a tamasic, inert, lot. The tamasic character is defined as one who never protests or is not moved even when he is kicked. The Buddha, he asserted, ruined India in this respect. It was the efforts of Kumarilla, Shankara and Ramanuja that put India back on the path of action.[126] Vivekananda found the idea of turning the other cheek 'impossible, impracticable!'[127] He felt that this form of ethic was meant for people whose aim in life was righteousness and perfection. For ordinary men, loving one's enemy was untenable.[128] If they did so, they would be driven out by those who believed in the 'might is right' principle.

Forgiveness too ought not to be passive and weak. Vivekananda resorted to the example of Arjuna pleading with Krishna to forgive his enemies to present his view. Paraphrasing Krishna's answer in his own, inimitable way he said: 'You speak the words of a wise man, but you are not a wise man, but a coward.'[129] The Swami was once asked whether one ought to court death in defence of what is right, or ought one to follow the lesson of the Gita and be unmoved, be a sthitaprajna—be like a realized individual who was perfectly calm, not given to anger, temptations and attachment. This was a parallel reading of the Gita and Vivekananda's reply is extremely significant: 'I am for no reaction,' said the Swami, speaking slowly and with a long pause. Then he added '—for Sannyasins. Self-defence for the householder!'[130] Retaliatory violence, or to use the word popularly used by contemporary followers of jihadi Hindutva, namely, pratishodh, was built into the project of transforming Hinduism into a macho faith. Vivekananda contributed in equal measure to the idea of Hinduism as an aggressive and martial faith. Ironically, this idea of Hinduism went hand in hand with Vivekananda's belief in the salience of the 'mild Hindu' ideal.

Making Hindus more 'manly' was just one detail in the way of emancipating India. This, however, was not India's unique mission in the world. Vivekananda defines this mission by way of an analogy. Just as every human being possesses individuality, so do nations.[131] Races constitute nations. Individuals differ from each other and so do races. There is something called the economy of nature which impels every individual and race alike to fulfil a certain purpose, a karma. Like individuals, nations and races have a destiny to fulfil, a message to deliver and a mission to accomplish. Nations and races define this ultimate goal differently.

Every nation has a point 'where the life of a nation centres'.[132] This is where the nationality of a nation lies. As long as this 'centre' is allowed to remain untouched, the nation survives and cannot be assailed by external threats. Vivekananda was clear that the 'centre' in India's case was religion:

> In India, religious life forms the centre, the keynote of the whole music of national life; and if any nation attempts to throw off its national vitality, the direction which has become its own through the transmission of centuries,—that nation dies, if it succeeds in the attempt.[133]

The Hindu race and the Hindu nation had preserved this 'centre' by withstanding foreign invasions and religious persecution. The salvation of India lay in preserving this centre as their forefathers had done:

> Temple after temple was broken down by the foreign conqueror, but no sooner had the wave passed than the spire of the temple rose again. Some of these old temples of Southern India, and those like Somanatha of Gujerat, will teach you volumes of wisdom, will give you a keener insight into the history of the race than any amount of books. Mark how these temples bear the marks of a hundred attacks and a hundred regenerations, continually destroyed and continually springing up out of the ruins, rejuvenated and strong as ever! That is the national mind, that is the national life-current.[134]

Sciences, says Vivekananda, can feed people, help conquer others, establish one's rule over others and enable the strong to domineer over others. The Hindus could have excelled in discovering this unique gift of science, but instead, they discovered 'the other side',[135] namely religion. This was the national 'core'. The Hindu and religion had become synonymous. The Muslims had invaded India, yet the Hindus had survived this and were ready to face such eventualities in the future. They managed to preserve the 'core'.

> Barbarians with sword and fire, barbarians bringing barbarous religions, not one of them could touch the core, not one could touch the 'jewel', not one had the power to kill the 'bird' which the soul of the race inhabited. This, therefore, is the vitality of the race, and so long as that remains there is no power under the sun that can kill the race.[136]

In short, all that the Hindus wanted was spiritual independence. As long as religious freedom remained untouched, the Hindu even tolerated slavery.[137] The invading Pathans tried to interfere with religion and were unsuccessful in building an empire in India. The initial strength of the Mughal Empire resided in leaving religion untouched. Jehangir, Shahjahan and Dara Shukoh were, says Vivekananda, after all born of Hindu mothers. But the moment Aurangzeb tried to touch the 'core', the empire itself vanished. Vivekananda argued in favour of keeping 'that one gate of religion free and unmolested'.[138] Under the ashes of apparent death, said Vivekananda, the fire of national life was still smouldering.

For Vivekananda, what was this life of the nation? Religion. What was the language of the nation? Religion. What was the central idea of this nation? Religion. Politics, society, poverty alleviation and social reform had to be approached only through religion. India's 'core' was not politics or social reform, but religion. It was the religion of the Aryans. Like Savarkar after him, Vivekananda had to wrestle with the term 'Hindu' at the very outset.[139] At one time the epithet 'Hindu' signified those people who lived on the eastern shores, and beyond, of the Indus. Vivekananda persisted that the religion of those living on this side of the Indus was no longer homogeneous. The word 'Hindu', in its geographical sense, no longer covered only the Hindus as it was originally meant to, but also Muslims, Christians, Jains and members of many other religious persuasions. Vivekananda preferred to use the name 'Vaidiks', followers of the Vedas, or 'Vedantists', followers of the Vedanta, for the Hindus instead.[140] The term 'Hindu' for him had lost all its meaning. Nevertheless, the challenge to impart a sense of coherence and content to the 'core' remained.

The first impediment in Vivekananda's path was the idea of dualism.[141] In India, and all over the world, dualism had triumphed. The vast number of Indians were dualists, so were 90 per cent of the population of the earth, including all European and West Asian religions. What was originally proposed as the exclusive vice of other religions had now become the primary foe of Hinduism itself. Dualism invariably won, said Vivekananda, because it appealed to the less educated mind.[142] Ordinary human beings could not conceive of an idea that is not concrete. To teach dualism in India was a great mistake.[143] People found the process towards understanding 'ultimate principles' very intricate and got alarmed. Instead, they took refuge in dualism. What was so diabolical about dualism? Vivekananda felt that dualism weakened the mind, made people superstitious, made them desire all sorts of wild impossibilities and mysteries.[144]

Vivekananda, then, went on to offer an elaborate typology of dualists and dualism, classified broadly into Vedantic and non-Vedantic dualists.[145] While the details of each of these classifications are interesting in themselves, it would suffice to quote Vivekananda's formal definition of dualism for the sake of the present argument.

> The Dualists believe that God, who is the Creator of the universe and its Ruler, is eternally separate from Nature, eternally separate from the human soul. God is eternal; Nature is eternal; so are all souls. Nature and the souls become manifested and change, but God remains the same. According to the Dualists, again, this God is personal, in that He has qualities, not that He has a body. He has human attributes; He is merciful; He is just; He is powerful; He is almighty; He can be approached; He can be prayed to; He can be loved; He loves in return, and so forth. In one word, He is a human God, only infinitely greater than man; He has none of the evil qualities which men have. 'He is the repository of an infinite number of blessed qualities,' that is their definition. He cannot create without materials, and Nature is the material out of which He creates the whole universe.[146]

Endowing God with human qualities led to one form or the other of exclusiveness. Dualistic religions and sects quarrelled with each other due to this sense of exclusiveness. To perceive God as an abstract idea is difficult for the lower intellect. Ordinary people liked to believe in a God who is separate from them, a mighty monarch, but purer than the earthly kings. They, then, ascribed all the good qualities to God and removed any trace of evil from him. The idea of a personal god led to a proliferation of sects swearing fidelity to their own notions of one.

Only a grand and timeless ideal could hold together the 'centre' or the 'core' and save it from the challenge posed by dualism. Sects within Hinduism had to be woven together into a single tapestry. Hinduism also had to define its relationship with other dualistic religions. The solution had to provide for diversity, and at the same time forge a viable unity. Vivekananda had already taken the first step in this direction by suggesting that Hinduism was a tolerant and universal faith. His propagation of the idea that all faiths ultimately lead towards the same goal was certainly a beginning. But this was not sufficient to calm passions in favour of a plethora of personal gods, sacred texts, customs and superstitions. The 'core' had to be cast in a solid mould.

In a letter written on 20 June 1894, Vivekananda provides the key to his restatement of Hinduism. '[O]ld Hinduism,' he writes, 'can only be reformed through Hinduism.'[147] What was old Hinduism? It was that religion which preached lofty ideals of human dignity on the one hand, and 'treads upon the necks of the poor and the low'.[148] When Vivekananda spoke of 'old' Hinduism, he did not mean 'ancient' Hinduism. Similarly, when he talked about 'modern' Hinduism, he did imply the Hinduism he took upon himself to reform. Both terms—'old' and 'modern'—were used in a pejorative sense. They simply referred to the form of Hinduism based on the Puranas. The Puranas, he asserts, were produced by men of limited intelligence, were full of errors, fallacies and feeling of class and malice.[149] These had to be rejected.

The Vedas were the only force that had the capacity to unify all sects within Hinduism. Vivekananda calls them the scriptures of the Hindus.[150] The Vedic religion was universal and all-embracing. They were the only scriptures that contained the notion of an absolute God. All other notions of God—personal God, almighty God or God in heaven—were merely 'minimised and limited versions'[151] of God. The nameless, limitless and eternal Vedic religion not only unified all manner of sects in India but also contained within it the essence and possibilities of all other religions of the world.[152] For a Hindu, fidelity to the Vedas was absolute and unconditional:

> This perhaps is certain, that no man can have a right to be called a Hindu who does not admit the supreme authority of the Vedas.[153]

Having established the unquestioned supremacy of the Vedas, Vivekananda divided the Vedas into two distinct portions. The first was the karma kanda portion, which contained knowledge about various rituals, ceremonies and sacrifices. These, he said, had fallen into disuse in the present times.[154] The other portion dealt with jnana kanda, which concerned itself with the spiritual teachings of the Vedas. This latter portion he calls the Upanishads and the Vedanta.[155] In other words, the Upanishads contained the essence as well as the summit of Vedic knowledge.

Vivekananda further refined the idea of what constituted 'scriptures' for the Hindus. 'The Upanishads,' he says, 'are our Scriptures.'[156] The compulsion to identify a text or a set of texts was extreme for Vivekananda. Hinduism had to contend with all other religions that were faith-based on an identifiable text. The 'core' could not be secured without naming a text for the Hindus.

> You must remember that what the Bible is to the Christians, what the Quran is to the Mohammedans, what the Tripitaka is to the Buddhists, what the Zend Avesta is to the Parsis, these Upanishads are to us. These and nothing but these are our Scriptures.[157]

In India, Vivekananda argued, there was a proliferation of local customs that assumed the status of orthodoxy. Often, karma kanda supplanted the authority of the Upanishads. These local customs and observances often were the sole arbiters of the Hindu identity. Vivekananda would have none of this. The status of the Upanishads was immutable and non-negotiable.

> Manu, and the Puranas, and all other books are to be taken so far as they agree with the authority of the Upanishads, and when they disagree they are to be rejected without mercy.[158]

The Upanishads were, therefore, the primary and only authority. To be a Hindu was to subordinate oneself to their sovereign authority. Any Hindu, asserted Vivekananda, who denied the authority of the Vedas and the Upanishads was a non-believer, a nastika.[159] A true Hindu was one who subordinated everything to spirituality and the purity of the race.[160] To deny the Upanishads was to deny the very basis of one's identity.

Having established Vedantic determinism, Vivekananda moved a step further. He said that the scriptures of all other religions were merely Puranas. This is because they describe the history of the deluge, the history of kings and their families, and the lives of great men. They were not timeless, unwritten and eternal like the Vedas. Their core had been sullied by human intervention and history. Hence, their validity and legitimacy were dependent on their moral teachings concurring with the authority of the Vedas and the Upanishads.[161] If these scriptures were to contradict the tenets of Vedanta, they had to be mercilessly rejected. Even if elements within these scriptures agreed with the Vedas, they would still not qualify to be called scriptures in the same way as the Vedas were; they would still remain Puranas.

The superiority of Vedanta rested on the fact that it contained, not merely all religions, but all of religion itself.[162] The very idea of religion corresponded to the three stages of Vedanta philosophy, i.e., dvaita, dualism; vishishtadvaita, qualified monism; and advaita, monism. Each of these three stages is indeed a stage in the spiritual growth of man and each of these is necessary. Christianity and Islam fell into the category of dvaita, the first stage. Advaita applied in its 'yoga-perception form'[163] was Buddhism. In India, Vedanta circumscribed dualism, qualified monism and monism in equal measure. Even Buddhism and Jainism in India borrowed heavily from the Upanishads, though they were reluctant to admit the fact.[164]

Vivekananda, then, introduced an additional nuance in his quest for Vedantic determinism. Having stated the superior claims of Vedanta, and having equated Vedanta with an all-embracing notion of religion itself, he went on to call advaita 'the fairest flower of philosophy and religion that any country in any age has produced'.[165] The merit of advaita lay in its acceptance of dualism. The advaitin did not deny dualism but perceived it only as a lower form of religion. In other words, advaita denied the divisive notion of individuality. Human beings were constantly changing. There was no individuality, persisted Vivekananda, in case of the body, or mind, or even thought. These were ever in a state of flux. Is there anything that lies beyond the contingent notions of body, mind and thought?

> [B]eyond that is your Atman, and says the Advaitist, this Atman is the Brahman Itself. There cannot be two Infinites. There is only one individual and it is Infinite. In plain words, we are rational beings, and we want to reason. And what is reason? More or less of classification, until you cannot go on any further. And the finite can only find its ultimate rest when it is classified into the Infinite.[166]

In other words, advaita goes beyond persons, sects, texts, dogmas and notions of personal god. At the same time it allows the full play of individuals and their infinite variations. Indeed, Advaita Vedanta asserts that all human beings are divine.

> You are all Gods. One God is not sufficient. You are all Gods, says the Vedanta.[167]

IV

Vivekananda interpreted Hinduism for the West as a tolerant, universal faith. It was portrayed as the mother of all religions from whom other religions had much to learn. For the purpose of reviving the Hindu nation, he privileged the Vedas and the Upanishads, and made the absolute authority of Vedanta as the foundation upon which to unify faith. There is, however, a third version of Hinduism that Vivekananda formulated which transcends the limitations of the first two interpretations. This was his 'private' Hinduism, though he was often vocal about its defining features. To understand this 'private' version, certain elements from it need to be stated immediately.

Societies, Vivekananda felt, ought to be moulded upon truth. Those societies where the highest truths become practical are the greatest.[168] Advaita would be meaningful only when it is made practical. It was not enough to attain personal liberation through advaita. In pursuing personal liberation, the effort should be to also liberate the whole universe.[169]

> And why am I here? Only the sight of the country's misery and the thought of its future do not let me remain quiet any more!—Even Samadhi and all that appears as futile—even the sphere of Brahma with its enjoyments becomes insipid! My vow of life is to think of your welfare.[170]

Vivekananda rejected Shankara's idea that all work was essentially the result of ignorance. This proposition might be true from an absolute standpoint, but work had great utility in the world. Vivekananda went a step further and suggested that once the atman was realized, performing actions or not performing them ultimately came under the control of the realized individual. In that state all actions led towards good work for the well-being of human beings in the world.[171]

Still more forcefully Vivekananda articulated the point about Practical Vedanta. In his love for God, man had forgotten to love his fellow beings. This love of God induced him often enough to give up his own life; and frequently kill other human beings in the name of God. Nations were robbed and the earth was covered with human blood for the greater glory of God. The time had come to turn to the 'other God',[172] namely, the human being. In India too, the real nation that lived in the humble village hut had been forgotten.[173] The common people in India had suffered oppression for thousands of years. They had withstood this without a murmur, with infinite patience, boundless love and immense practicality. They were the real heroes of India.[174] Their state had a lot to do with the 'tyranny of the sages'.[175] For thousands of years, the 'proletariat'[176] had been prevented from bettering their lot by barriers built by 'the tyranny of the great, tyranny of the spiritual, tyranny of the intellectual, tyranny of the wise'.[177]

The first logical step towards Practical Vedanta was to recognize the primacy of food. Vivekananda wanted the cry for food to end in India. He exhorted Indians to adopt Western science and 'dig the earth and produce foodstuff'.[178] People ought to throw the scriptures in the Ganga and exert themselves in procuring food and clothing instead. Only after that is done, would reading the scriptures have some meaning.

> I do not believe in a God or religion which cannot wipe the widow's tears or bring a piece of bread to the orphan's mouth. However sublime be the theories, however well-spun may be the philosophy—I do not call it religion so long as it is confined to books and dogmas.[179]

Hindus were particularly unfit for approximating to Practical Vedanta. Vivekananda gives reasons for this in the form of a searing indictment of Hinduism:

> We have brains, but no hands. We have the doctrine of Vedanta, but we have not the power to reduce it into practice. In our books there is the doctrine of universal equality, but in work we make great distinctions. It was in India that unselfish and disinterested work of the most exalted type was preached, but in practice we are awfully cruel, awfully heartless—unable to think anything besides our own mass-of-flesh bodies.[180]

Hindus lacked all those things that made nations great: Conviction of the powers of goodness, absence of jealousy and suspicion and helping those who are trying to be and do good.[181] Vivekananda lists jealousy as the single most significant reason for the Hindu nation falling to pieces.

Having cast aside much of his own formal redefinition of Hinduism in favour of Practical Vedanta, Vivekananda had to make the Practical Vedanta ideal work. Clearly, he did not think that Hinduism, however interpreted, could give a helping hand in realizing this ideal. Looking upon all mankind as one's own soul was an attribute underdeveloped among the Hindus. In a letter written on 10 June 1889, Vivekananda felt that 'without the help of practical Islam, theories of Vedantism, however fine and wonderful they may be, are entirely valueless to the vast mass of mankind'.[182] Islam had shown the way towards a practical ideal of brotherhood and equality.

> For our own motherland a junction of the two great systems, Hinduism and Islam—Vedanta brain and Islam body—is the only hope.
>
> I see in my mind's eye the future perfect India rising out of this chaos and strife, glorious and invincible, with Vedanta brain and Islam body.[183]

Ramakrishna's 'mandate' had helped Vivekananda surmount the problem of giving content to the idea of Practical Vedanta.

> And together [Vivekananda and a few other disciples of Sri Ramakrishna] we conceived that this ideal had to be spread. And not only spread, but made practical. That is to say, we must show the spirituality of the Hindus, the mercifulness of the Buddhists, the activity of the Christians, the brotherhood of the Mohammedans by our practical lives.[184]

Sri Ramakrishna's love had unified all sects and religions. He had removed all distinctions; all had a share in the Divine Love. He was the harbinger of the Satyayuga, the

Golden Age of Truth.[185] He had shown the way to realize Practical Vedanta.

While theoretically Vedanta embraced all religions and contained their essence, earlier Vivekananda had posited an evolutionary schema of development of different faiths. Hinduism had scaled the heights of perfection whereas other religions were still evolving. Vivekananda's Practical Vedanta was a blow even to his own highly purified redefinition of Hinduism. Practical Vedanta had privileged bread over God, the 'proletariat' in preference to the Brahmins, service over the tyranny of the wise and love over the absolute authority of the Upanishads. Islam and Christianity were no longer barbarian faiths, mired in dualism, but equal partners in the realization of Practical Vedanta. Buddhism was no longer the destroyer of Vedic religion. A curious inversion had taken place.

This was Vivekananda's 'private' Hinduism. It had been achieved through supreme devotion, para-bhakti, where the love of God transcends everything. In Vivekananda's case, this love had to be directed towards the 'other God', the human being.

> That love of God grows and assumes a form which is called Para-Bhakti, or supreme devotion. Forms vanish, rituals fly away, books are superseded, images, temples, churches, religions and sects, countries and nationalities, all these little limitations and bondages fall off by their own nature from him who knows this love of God. Nothing remains to bind him or fetter his freedom.[186]

There was precious little within orthodox Hinduism

to help translate para-bhakti into the requirements of Practical Vedanta. Yet, Hinduism was on the verge of dissolution under the pressure exerted by Practical Vedanta. For all practical purposes, Vedanta might have been a Hindu coinage, but in its practical manifestation it bore no resemblance to its parent faith. Neither was it pure monism either, for, in that, the question of service, brotherhood and mercifulness did not arise. Vivekananda did try to justify Practical Vedanta by reinterpreting Shankara, as shown above, but the justification still falls short of saving appearances for Hinduism as a faith.

Vivekananda had contemptuously likened modern Hinduism to a form of 'stranded Buddhism'.[187] He believed that Hinduism, with all its ugliness, had to be reformed through Hinduism alone. Practical Vedanta was sparse and bare-boned. It had removed the clutter of scriptures, sects, varnadharma, ashramadharma, dogmas, rituals, identity of faiths and even nationality from the question of religion. Vivekananda was personally attracted to Practical Vedanta. At the same time, as a religious preacher and a nationalist he could not afford to see Hinduism withering away. In the end, it was Vivekananda's engagement with Buddhism that brought about a reconciliation between Practical Vedanta and his version of Hinduism representing absolute adherence to the Vedas and the Upanishads as shown in Part III.

Speaking at the Parliament of Religions on 20 September 1893, Vivekananda pronounced that the Buddha had not preached anything new.[188] Like Christ, the Buddha had come to fulfil and not to destroy. What had he come to fulfil? According to Vivekananda, these were the truths of the Hindu religion, nothing more. The Buddha was the logical conclusion of the development of Hinduism. Buddha's disciples had not understood his message, and as a consequence, distorted it. In this early formulation, Vivekananda gave little credit to the Buddha or his teachings, but there is recognition of the message of empathy taught by the Buddha. Having said this, Hinduism as a philosophy was still infinitely superior.

> Hinduism cannot live without Buddhism, nor Buddhism without Hinduism. Then realize what the separation has shown to us, that the Buddhists cannot stand without the brain and philosophy of the Brahmins, nor the Brahmin without the heart of the Buddhist. This separation between the Buddhists and the Brahmins is the cause of the downfall of India.[189]

Buddhism, he says, is a great religion in many respects, but it ought not to be confused with Vedanta. The difference between Buddhism and Vedanta was similar to the difference between Christianity and the Salvation Army.[190] This was Vivekananda's early position on Buddhism.

For many years, Vivekananda's lectures and writings refused to grant Buddhism either originality or worth. The Swami was emphatic that Buddhism was derivative of the Upanishads. Even the 'so-called great and wonderful ethics of Buddhism'[191] were to be found verbatim in the Upanishads. Buddhism was merely a sect of Hinduism.

In a lecture delivered in Detroit, Vivekananda called Buddhism 'one of our sects'.[192] He, then, proceeded to describe the Buddha and the founding of Buddhism.

> It was founded by a great man called Gautama, who became disgusted at the eternal metaphysical discussions of his day, and the cumbrous rituals, and more especially with the caste system. Some people say that we are born to a certain state, and therefore we are superior to others who are not thus born. He was also against the tremendous priestcraft. He preached a religion in which there was no motive power, and was perfectly agnostic about metaphysics or theories about God. He was often asked if there was a God, and he answered he did not know. When asked about right conduct he would reply—Do good and be good.[193]

Vivekananda acknowledged that it was possible for a man like the Buddha to attain to the highest levels of spirituality without the aid of belief in God, metaphysics, sect or temple. He also envied the enormous empathy of the Buddha. But this did not mean a complete endorsement of all of his philosophy. Vivekananda at this juncture wanted 'a good deal of metaphysics'[194] for himself.

Despite this qualified endorsement of the Buddha and the faith he founded, Vivekananda could not bring himself to accept Buddhism wholeheartedly. On the contrary, he found nothing right in Buddhism at this juncture. Buddha was not the destroyer of Brahminical idolatry but its creator.[195] Buddha made the mistake of identifying caste as a religious institution and tried to destroy it. Buddhism disrupted the ancient equilibrium that existed between the Kshatriyas and the Brahmins. Buddha also committed the error of introducing an extremely negative iconoclasm which was later corrected by Shankara, Madhava and Ramanuja.[196] This error was further compounded by the use of popular languages by the Buddhists in lieu of Sanskrit; this created a dangerous rupture from the Vedic tradition.[197] The Buddhist tenet of non-killing being a supreme virtue brought ruin upon India.[198] In formulating it, Buddhism paid little heed to the capacities of people and their contexts. The Buddha might have exhibited tremendous mercy and lack of personal motives in preaching his ideas, but the faith that he inaugurated was rotten through and through.

> Thus, inspite of the preaching of mercy to animals, in spite of the sublime ethical religion, in spite of the hair-splitting discussions about the existence or non-existence of a permanent soul, the whole building of Buddhism tumbled down piecemeal; and the ruin was simply hideous. I have neither the time nor the inclination to describe to you the hideousness that came in the wake of Buddhism. The most hideous ceremonies, the most horrible, the most obscene books that human hands ever wrote or the human brain ever conceived, the most bestial forms that ever passed under the name of religion, have all been the creation of degraded Buddhism.[199]

Buddhism, in short, had inherent flaws, that got further accentuated in its degraded state.

Vivekananda's discomfort with Buddhism persisted as long as he defined Hinduism as the 'core' or the 'centre' of national life. At a superficial level, Vivekananda questioned Buddha's authority to challenge the Vedas, even though the challenge, he admitted, was largely directed at the ritualistic aspects of the Vedas.[200] In the same breath there was also the assertion that Buddhism stood on the foundation of Vedanta; that many of the conclusions of the Buddhists were derived from advaita.[201] The points of difference between Buddhism and Hinduism, however, were more fundamental.

> Buddha is expressly agnostic about God; but God is everywhere preached in our religion. The Vedas teach God—both personal and impersonal. God is everywhere preached in the Gita. Hinduism is nothing without God. The Vedas are nothing without Him. That is the only way to salvation. Sannyasins have to repeat the following, several times: I, wishing for mukti, take refuge in God, who created the world, who breathed out the Vedas.[202]

In other words, Buddhism had tried to tamper with the 'core'. The ultimate consequence was the expulsion of Buddhism from India.

Practical Vedanta had no such quarrel with Buddhism. Vivekananda now saw Buddhism with new eyes. It was no longer a destroyer of the Vedas but a reformer of the Vedic religions by standing against ceremonials, animal sacrifices, hereditary caste, exclusive priesthood and belief in permanent souls. Neither did Buddhism attempt to overturn the social order.[203] Buddha too fared far better than before in this altered perspective.

> What Buddha did was to break wide open the gates of that very religion which was confined in the Upanishads to a particular caste. What special greatness does his theory of Nirvana confer on him? His greatness lies in

> his unrivalled sympathy. The high orders of Samadhi, etc., that lend gravity to his religion, are almost all there in the Vedas; what are absent there are his intellect and heart, which have never since been paralleled throughout the history of the world.[204]

Even Shankara did not have the slightest bit of Buddha's heart and dry intellect. Vivekananda blames Shankara for resorting to sophistry in order to prove that the scriptures, after all, did uphold the tenets of his philosophy.[205] Not so the Buddha. The Buddha was much more brave and sincere. He gave the world the first complete system of morality. He was good to all and he loved all without a motive. His message was simple: 'Believe no book; the Vedas are all humbug. If they agree with me, so much the better for the books. I am the greatest book; sacrifices and prayers are useless.'[206] Vivekananda called the Buddha the George Washington of religions: He conquered a throne only to give it to the people.[207]

Buddha was brave and sincere. He also had an unrivalled heart. But this was not all. He was a great Vedantin. Before his appearance, religion was reducible to a few principles recorded on palm leaves which were known only to a few. 'It was the Lord Buddha,' says Vivekananda, 'who brought them down to the practical field, and showed how to apply them in the everyday life of the people.'[208] The Buddha was the living embodiment of Practical Vedanta. He too was Naradeva Deva like Sri Ramakrishna.

On 18 March 1900, a couple of years before his death, Vivekananda gave a lecture in San Francisco titled 'Buddha's Message to the World'.[209] This lecture was less an exposition of Buddha's message and more a manifesto of Vivekananda's doctrine of Practical Vedanta. Vivekananda maintained that the Buddha taught the gist of Vedic philosophy, but he taught this true spirituality to all without distinction of caste, creed or sect. He opened the doors of Nirvana for all.

> He had the brain, the power, and the heart—a heart as infinite as the broad sky. He felt how the masses were being led by the priests and how the priests were glorying in their power, and he wanted to do something about it. He did not want any power over anyone, and he wanted to break the mental and spiritual bonds of men. His heart was large. The heart, many around us may have, and we also want to help others. But we do not have the brain; we do not know the ways and means by which help can be given. But this man had the brain to discover the means of breaking the bondages of the soul. He learnt why men suffer, and he found the way out of suffering. He was a man of accomplishment, he worked everything out; he taught one and all without distinction and made them realize the peace of enlightenment.[210]

India, the land of religion and spirituality, found the Buddha's message too audacious. It shocked the people. They found its radicalism too hard to swallow.

Vivekananda puts forth the reservations that Hindus had with Buddha's doctrine. He did so clinically, without taking sides. If any bias was evident, it was in favour of the Buddha. He began with the idea of centrality of God for Hinduism and the Buddha's denial of the existence of God:

> Hindus can give up everything except their God. To deny God is to cut off the very ground from under the feet of devotion. Devotion and God the Hindus must cling to. They can never relinquish these.[211]

In the Buddha's teachings there was no God and there was no soul either. So what was there in Buddhism?

> [S]imply work. What for? Not for the self, for the self is a delusion. We shall be ourselves when this delusion has vanished. Very few are there in the world that can rise to that height and work for work's sake.[212]

Buddha worked for work's sake. Vivekananda too wanted to work for work's sake. This was Practical Vedanta at its best.

All too aware of the danger of a complete surrender to the Buddha, Vivekananda was compelled to articulate Buddha's position from a Hindu standpoint. He had set out to discover for himself his 'private Hinduism'. The best manifestation of this was in the realm of Practical Vedanta. This did not, however, mean that Hinduism could be completely abandoned. Buddha's great doctrine of selflessness had to be legitimized by the authority of the Upanishads.

> In the Upanishads there is already the great doctrine of the Atman and the Brahman. The Atman, Self, is the same as Brahman, the Lord. This Self is all that is; It is the only reality. Maya, delusion, makes us see It as different. There is one Self, not many. That one Self shines in various forms. Man is man's brother because

> all men are one. A man is not only my brother, say the Vedas, he is myself. Hurting any part of the universe, I only hurt myself. I am the universe. It is a delusion that I think I am Mr. So-and-So—that is delusion.[213]

Buddha's doctrine of equality and brotherhood could be justified through recourse to the Upanishads, but it still left the idea of 'work' a bit unhinged. Vivekananda returned to the Buddha's teachings through a curious detour. While retaining the idea of God within Hinduism, Vivekananda made common cause with the Buddha in damning the 'prevalent ideas of God'.[214] These notions of God made men weak and superstitious.

> If you pray to God to give you everything, who is it, then, that goes out and works? God comes to those who work hard. God helps them that help themselves. An opposite idea of God weakens our nerves, softens our muscles, makes us dependent.[215]

The equation was simple: Everything independent is happy; everything dependent is miserable.

Like Buddha, Vivekananda wanted to be selfless, bold, fearless and loving. He attempted to realize this through the construction of his 'private Hinduism'. The instrumentality of Practical Vedanta freed him of the weight of tradition, customs, dogmas, sects, scriptures and doctrines. Yet, he could never abandon the idea of God. In his articulation of 'private' Hinduism, the only Hindu entity that still made him dependent was his devotion to the idea of God. He never took the Buddha's leap in denying God. The fragility of the Practical Vedanta ideal exasperated Vivekananda. Also, he remained torn between contending notions of Hinduism all his life, some of which were his creation.

Vivekananda's agony in making sense of Hinduism mirrors the trauma of contemporary India too. The Ksheer Bhavani temple story is well known.[216] During a visit to Srinagar, Vivekananda used to visit it every day. One day he was moved by the dilapidated state of the temple, which had been destroyed by Muslim invaders. He then heard Ksheer Bhavani telling him that the state of the temple was her will. If she wanted, she could erect a temple of gold for herself. She was his protector, not the other way round. The rebuff made Vivekananda contemplate giving up everything, including Practical Vedanta. Elsewhere, wearing his Vedantic cap, he had emphatically stated that 'temples have no hold on the Hindu religion; if they were all destroyed religion would not be affected a grain'.[217] Yet, a ruined temple moved him and made him despondent. In the battle between dualism and Practical Vedanta, Vivekananda remained a passionate participant and a sincere seeker.

VINAYAK DAMODAR SAVARKAR

Dayananda, Vivekananda and Aurobindo were men of religion, who also actively sought to restate Hinduism, reform Hindu society, and situate Hinduism in a national context. In contrast, Vinayak Damodar Savarkar had very little to do with matters of faith; yet, unlike anyone before or after him, Savarkar politicized religion and introduced religious metaphors into politics. He pioneered an extreme, uncompromising and rhetorical form of Hindu nationalism in Indian political discourse. His life exhibited an unwavering pursuit of a single ideal: to establish India as a Hindu nation. Even today, Savarkar remains the first, and most original, prophet of extremism in India.

In his biography of Savarkar,[1] Dhananjay Keer recounts an incident in which a twelve-year-old Vinayak Damodar Savarkar leads a march of his schoolmates to stone the village mosque. This was Savarkar's revenge against the 'atrocities' committed against Hindus during the Hindu–Muslim riots in Bombay and Pune in 1894-95 and earlier in Azamgarh in June 1893. Keer's gushing narrative of this incident speaks of the boys, led by

Savarkar, showering stones on the mosque, shattering its windows and tiles and returning triumphant.

Savarkar's own account of this act[2] speaks of his rage against the deeds of physical violence committed against the Hindus by Muslim rioters. (For him, it was always the Muslims who initiated a riot.) So, when Hindus killed Muslims in acts of retribution, Savarkar and his friends would dance with joy. These juvenile acts of revenge were ways of preserving the very existence of Hindu dharma and re-establishing national honour. Savarkar's description of raiding the mosque has a chilling echo to events of 6 December 1992:

> We vandalized the mosque to our heart's content and raised the flag of our bravery on it. We followed the war strategy of Shivaji completely and ran away from the site after accomplishing our task.[3]

The Muslim boys in the village retaliated but Savarkar and his band of 'dharmavir' warriors met the challenge with knives, pins and foot rulers. With unconcealed glee, Savarkar recounts the victory of the Hindus in this 'dharma yuddha', holy/righteous war.

Muslims as aggressors, the need for revenge, preserving Hindu dharma and securing national honour remained constant themes in Savarkar's life and thought. His writings are replete with terms like pratishodh and pratikaar, all synonyms for revenge, retribution and retaliation—not unlike the utterances of the BJP, the VHP, the Bajrang Dal, Narendra Modi and Praveen Togadia.

As the progenitor and most eloquent theoretician of political Hindutva, Savarkar formulated his entire world-view in terms of well-entrenched, non-negotiable, binary oppositions. His universe is strictly divided into 'friends' and 'foes', 'us' and 'them', 'Hindus' and 'Muslims', 'Hindus' and 'non-Hindus', 'righteous' and 'wicked'. In a rare advaitic vein—for Savarkar had little time for philosophic schools of Hinduism and was deeply suspicious of advaita—he talks of the nature of the Self as something that was 'known to itself immutably and without a name or even a form'.[4] This abstract notion of the Self, however, gets transformed the moment 'it comes in contact or conflict with a non-self'.[5] At this juncture the Self requires a name in order to communicate with the non-self.

The Self and the non-self in Savarkar's case were invariably in conflict and in an antagonistic relation. In his scheme of things, it was inconceivable for the Self and the non-self to share a creative and happy relationship. The more Savarkar engaged in formulating the contours of his ideal of Hindutva and giving it a political edge, the greater was the proliferation of the non-selves. Islam and 'Mohammadans' constituted the primary definition of the non-self. Later, it was the English and Christianity. Curiously enough, the Buddha and Buddhism and Mahatma Gandhi and ahimsa were eventually added to his rogue's gallery of non-selves.

Apologists of Savarkar's brand of Hindutva have often argued that all his utterances ought to be seen in the context of Indian nationalism in the nineteenth and twentieth centuries. They maintain that Savarkar should be viewed as a patriot and a revolutionary nationalist determined to secure India's freedom from the British.

While Savarkar was certainly part of the nationalist movement, his commitment to the creation of a Hindu Rashtra superseded the goal of political independence for India. The very definition and conception of Hindu Rashtra depended entirely on its relation with its primary non-self, the Muslims.

Before the Muslims invaded India—Savarkar uses the words Hindusthan or Sindhusthan or Saptasindhu—it was a land of peace, plenty and a sense of false security. There were internal differences of regions, identities and castes but these were welded together in a great synthesis, a tremendous 'mahamilan'.[6] The coming of the Muslims disturbed this idyllic picture:

> At last she was rudely awakened on the day when Mohammed of Gazni crossed the Indus, the frontier line of Sindhusthan, and invaded her. That day the conflict of life and death began. Nothing makes [the] Self conscious of itself so much as a conflict with [the] non-self. Nothing can weld peoples into a nation and nations into a state as the pressure of a common foe. Hatred separates as well as unites.[7]

Savarkar saw this as a ghastly conflict that continued 'day after day, decade after decade, century after century' till such time as Shivaji established a Hindu Empire, a Hindu-Pad-Padashahi.

The conflict with the mlechchhas and Yavanas—the outcastes and 'outsiders'—defined Hindu identity and constituted the Hindus as a nation. In the course of this conflict, 'our people became intensely conscious of ourselves as Hindus and we were welded into a nation to an extent unknown in our history'.[8] What brought about this unity was the presence of the 'enemy':

> The enemies hated us as Hindus and the whole family of peoples and races, of sects and creeds that flourished from Attock to Cuttack was suddenly individualized into a single Being ... For it was one great issue to defend the honour and independence of Hindusthan and maintain the cultural unity and civic life of Hindutva and not Hinduism alone, but Hindutva—i.e., Hindudharma—that was being fought out on the hundred fields of battle as well as on the floor of the chambers of diplomacy.[9]

All territory from the River Attock to the Indian Ocean was to be freed from the hands of the Muslims. The goal of the Hindus was the same as that of Shivaji: Reacquire territory, rehabilitate religion, preserve the Vedas and shastras, protect cows and Brahmins, establish suzerainty and diffusion of Hindu fame and glory. These were the sentiments expressed in a letter Govindrao Kale wrote to Nana Fadnavis, which for Savarkar was the truest expression of Hindu history.

There are various ways to understand Savarkar's attitude towards the Muslims. There are several instances in his works where this 'struggle of life and death with the Muhammadan power' is relegated to merely a question of remembering the past and documenting it truthfully. In his author's foreword to *Hindu-Pad-Padashahi,* Savarkar sports an extremely liberal attitude when he says, 'It would be as suicidal and as ridiculous to borrow hostilities and combats of the past only to fight them out into the present, as it would be for a Hindu and a Muhammadan to lock each other suddenly in a death-grip while embracing, only because Shivaji and Afzal Khan had done so hundreds of years ago.'[10] The anti-Muslim rhetoric after 1937 can also be seen as a reaction to Congress politics and the politics of the Muslim League. None of these instances, however, explain sufficiently Savarkar's obsessive preoccupation with Islam and the Muslims.

The truth is that Savarkar greatly admired the Muslims. For him, they represented all that was deficient or missing in the Hindus. While Savarkar would remain committed to a Hindu God or Dev, and a Hindu Rashtra or Desh, he greatly admired the political and religious fervour of Islam. In *Hindu-Pad-Padashahi,* subtitled *A Review of the Hindu Empire of Maharashtra*, Savarkar speaks about the first Muslim invasions in India:

> At the time of the first inroads of the Muhamadans, the fierce unity of Faith, that social cohesion and valorous fervour which made them as a body so irresistible, were qualities in which the Hindus proved woefully wanting.[11]

He goes on to praise the single-mindedness of Muslim religiosity and sense of solidarity:

> [I]t must be clearly mentioned that in whatever manner the absolute merits or demerits of a militant church be judged from the point of view of expansion of political and religious conquests, the community that is out for the propagation of their faith and is taught the fierce doctrines of believing other religions as passports to

> hell and all efforts to root out these satanic strongholds by force or fraud as highly meritorious is, other things being equal, better fitted to fight and vanquish its opponents and rule over them when opposed to a community which belongs not to a militant church at all, condemns the use of force, nay going further, would not like to receive back into its fold even those who were forcibly carried away from its bosom, which prizes individual worship more than a public one and thus develops no organ or organization for a common defence of their faith as a church and which, lacking thus in the cohesion and the public strength that it engenders, fails to replace it by any other principle like love for the common motherland or, common race, or a common kingdom, or a state powerful enough to weld them all into an organic whole and render them dedicated to its defence and glory with as fierce a fervour as their opponents put forth.[12]

The Muslims possessed qualities that made them unassailable whereas the Hindus suffered limitations handed over to them by metaphysics and tradition:

> The Muhammadans when they came, found a source of irresistible strength in the principle of theocratic unity, indissolubly wedded to a sense of duty to reduce all the world to a sense of obedience to theocracy, an Empire under the direct supervision of God. The Hindus wedded to individual liberty and philosophic views of life and the ultimate cause of causes, fallen a prey to the most decentralizing and disabling institutions and superstitions, such as the one that prevented them from crossing their frontiers and thus threw them always on

> the defensive and whose political organizations were more personal than patriotic, had naturally from a national point of view degenerated into a congerie of small states bound together but very loosely by a sense of common civilization, were more conscious of the differences that divided them provincially, sectionally and religiously, than of the factors that bound them and marked them out as one people.[13]

The Hindus had to learn a great deal from them about building a commonly shared national life and consolidating the place of faith in their commonly shared lives:

> As an individual to an individual, the Hindu was as valorous and devoted to his faith as a Moslem. But community to a community, people to a people, the Muhammadans were fiercely united by a theocratic patriotism that incited them to do or die under the banner of their God and invested every effort to spread political rule over the unbelievers with the sanctity of a holy war. But as years and even centuries rolled by, the Hindus too learnt the bitter lesson and under the pressure of a common danger, became more conscious of those ties that united them as a people and marked them out as a nation than the factors that divided them. They too began to feel as Hindus first and everything else afterwards and sadly realized the weaknesses that had crept into their national life by an inherent tendency to isolate thought and action, a general lack of community of feeling and pride and national sympathy. Slowly they absorbed much that contributed to the success of the Muhammadans.[14]

It would be instructive here to recapitulate Savarkar's central thesis regarding what made the Muslims so 'irresistible'. The Muslims had a unified church, which was lacking in the Hindus. This made them better equipped to take on their opponents. They had a sense of community that ultimately helped in bringing about a sense of national unity. In sharp contrast, the Hindus were hopelessly divided in terms of schools of philosophy, debilitating metaphysical propositions, castes and a surfeit of conventions masquerading as tradition. Muslims acted under the direct command of God, had a notion of theocracy, which helped their militant campaigns against the kafirs. The Hindus were left to reconcile doctrines such as the Karma theory and principled opposition to use of force, all of which lead to a disjuncture between theory and practice.

In short, the Self had 'absorbed' a great deal of the non-self, leading it to redefine itself. The tormentors had proved to be teachers. A great deal of what Savarkar had learned from the Muslims would ultimately determine his conception of political Hindutva. He had to accept the brutal embrace of the intimate enemy.

While the Hindu Self had 'learned' and 'absorbed' several attributes of the non-self, it could not allow the non-self to emasculate its identity completely. The Self had to remain distinct and have an autonomy of its own. Having begun on a premise that Hindus were deficient in several respects when compared to Muslims, Savarkar now had the task of distancing himself from too close a comparison with the traditional adversary. After all, the

Hindus and Muslims were, according to him, locked in a life and death battle for centuries.

It was, therefore, important for Hindus to prove their strength and 'seek retribution for the wrongs done to them as a nation and a race'.[15] Any attempt to extend a hand of friendship to the Muslims, or accept a hand extended by the Muslims, had to be based on perfect equality. This, for Savarkar, was accomplished when the forces of 'Hindudom' entered Delhi triumphantly in 1761 and ensured that 'the Moslem throne and crown and standard lay hammered at the feet of Bhau and Vishvas'.[16] This event singularly heralded the possibility of an honourable unity between the Hindus and the Muslims. This would have been impossible, asserts Savarkar, without conquering the conqueror and dethroning the enthroned. But the principle was clear: No retribution, no friendship.

Savarkar's portrayal of the establishment in 1761 of Hindu-Pad-Padashahi, the Hindu Empire, was an instance of Hindus regaining a sense of self-possession and parity with Muslims. It was, however, only a theoretical possibility and remained firmly entrenched in the realm of history writing. In another instance of history writing, Savarkar came close to exhibiting that Hindus and Muslims, after all, were 'blood brothers'.[17]

His account of the War of Independence of 1857, written while he was in England, several years before Savarkar wrote *Hindu-Pad-Padashahi,* makes a strong case for 'feelings of mutual friendship'[18] between the Hindus and the Muslims. He started writing this extended essay in 1907. There is acknowledgement in it of the enmity between Hindus and Muslims but that is brushed aside as being 'born out of ignorance'.[19] In fact there are lyrical passages where Savarkar talks about members of the two antagonistic faiths partaking of the 'same milk of the breasts of the Motherland'[20] and becoming one. There is little in this text which prepares the reader to comprehend Savarkar's subsequent outbursts against the Muslims in works like *Hindutva* and in his speeches at the annual sessions of the Hindu Mahasabha.

Any proper understanding of Savarkar's conception of political Hindutva and his brand of cultural nationalism would remain incomplete without a proper analysis of his account of 1857. To understand all these strands of his thought, however, requires an account of Savarkar's understanding of Islam and its history in India. Despite qualifications like the ones mentioned above, it would not be incorrect to say that in so far as Islam remained the essential non-self, Savarkar's understanding of Islam in India remained unchanged from the time he pelted stones on a mosque in Bhagur as a twelve-year-old.

II

Savarkar's essay titled 'The Rise, Fall and Destruction of Muslim Theocracy'[21] begins very directly and unambiguously. Before Prophet Muhammad founded a new faith, his father, uncle and his Quraish tribe were all idol worshippers. After the new faith, Islam, was born, the Prophet and his followers were blamed by traditionalists of the Quraish tribe of breaking idols through secret raids conducted in Mecca. Having introduced the theme of idol breaking at the very outset, Savarkar returns to the theme again and again. After dwelling on how the new faith was founded—Muhammad declared himself a messenger of God and became the Prophet—Savarkar, in the same sequence, breathlessly, introduced his pet theme: 'This was followed by breaking of idols of the old faith.'[22]

Once this was accomplished, the Prophet was declared the political, religious and military head of his followers. Savarkar wanted to establish that Islam was founded on the strength of the sword and 'one who wields the sword has truth on his side' was to be the guiding principle of the new faith.[23] A lengthy discussion on the war of succession after the death of the Prophet is followed by an account of the emergence of the Shia and Sunni sects. This, for Savarkar, marked the end of unified Islam and the beginning of its disintegration. The emergence of the institutions of Khalifa for the Sunnis and that of the Imam for the Shias inaugurated violent contests for supremacy among the sects.

In tracing the growth of Islam, Savarkar cites the example of Khalifas ravaging their own holy places. The instance of Khalifa Abdul Malik destroying Mecca, he says, was similar to the destruction of Medina by Khalifa Yazid. In the course of these rivalries, mosques were converted into stables, whole cities were looted and thousands of Muslims were killed by fellow Muslims. Such savagery was aided and abetted by their blind love for their faith. What did all this illustrate? Savarkar was unambiguous in his conclusion:

> If these Muslims now reduce Parsi and Hindu places of worship to demonic distress, there is nothing surprising in it. They have been learning the lessons of

> savage religiosity and intolerant cruelty from the very inception of their religion.[24]

The onward march of Islam also meant conversion to Islam of the conquered people either willingly or under coercion. Savarkar stated that the sanction to enslave the men and women of the defeated state and distribute them among soldiers was granted to Muslims by the Prophet himself.[25] Women were distributed among soldiers as a form of reparation. This was, according to Savarkar, a way of ensuring a new generation in the Islamic faith.[26]

In his essay, 'Uprooting of Arab Culture from Turkey by Kemal Pasha',[27] Savarkar revisited his earlier arguments on the positive impact of Islam on India: its immense contribution to human progress through introducing a new philosophy, new religion and a novel style of architecture. The real contribution of Islam for Savarkar, however, was its combination of religion and the sword to conquer the world:

> Prophet Mohammad read the first aayat of the Qur'an Sharif and took his sword out from its sheath ... This civilization through its rule imprinted its religion, language, script, architecture and texts over large landmasses. This civilization not only clashed with the outmoded and decaying cultures of that period and gave them a new way of life, but also had a unique excellence and a new world-view, which made it conquer the world.[28]

Just as it had supplanted decaying and outmoded cultures and civilizations, Islam too, in turn, had become an unchanging and obsolete faith. This happened, according to Savarkar, the moment Islam clashed with modern European civilization.

In what follows, Savarkar delineated his theory of Time, change and progress, which also reflected his deep admiration for the modern technological and scientific civilization of Europe. As we shall discover later, these arguments cut both ways. They were intended as a critique of 'unchanging' and 'immutable' Islam and, at the same time, directed towards his project of uniting Hindus as a nation by attenuating the traditionally prior claims of Hinduism—Puranas, Bhakti movements, popular Hinduism, folk and tribal accretions—in favour of political Hindutva.

Nature, contended Savarkar, was ever geared towards progress. Similarly, it was difficult for humans to imprison Time. A book can be saved from termites by bringing out a new or improved edition, but to save a religious text or a holy book from the 'termite of Time' is impossible even for angels. The 'termite of Time' not only eats away the pages of such a text, but also devours its meaning and makes it irrelevant. It is impossible, therefore, to bring out an improved version of an unchanging and rigid religious text because such improvement is prohibited by that religion itself.[29] Islam and the Arab civilization it fostered was also smothered and prevented from progressing by an unchanging religious text.

Modern European civilization reduced the Arab civilization to a sorry state. Savarkar's admiration for modern civilization hinged on the fact that it changed with changing times. 'After the emergence of the scientific and technological age,' he says, 'this independent ancient civilization now wants to hold the reins of steam, electricity and radio waves and strike arrows of fire on the Moon in the high skies.'[30] It was this dynamism of modern civilization which made Islam powerless.

Kemal Pasha and the Young Turks understood the perils of clinging on to an outmoded and decaying civilization that would ultimately become an impediment in the path of progress. For Savarkar, progress was to be defined in terms of European nationalism, constitutional practices, science, technology, theories of governance and the military and social revolution all this had brought about.[31] Indian Muslims had failed to correctly read the writing on the wall: modern European civilization had made Islam obsolete.

Savarkar derived this theory of rise and decay of civilizations from an unlikely source. Herbert Spencer, writing during the middle of the nineteenth century, proposed a philosophy of evolution in which all phenomena of every kind were subject to the law of evolution. Spencer was greatly admired by Shyamji Krishna Varma, an early mentor of Savarkar. Spencer conceived of evolution as a law of progress. However, any stage of progress was temporary; it was subject to change and transformation. The history of the universe, therefore, obeyed a succession of cycles, or what Spencer calls alternate eras of evolution and dissolution. There was only one thing which was constant. Spencer calls this the 'persistence of force'. This was the sole agent of change, form and organization in the knowable universe.

*

It is important at this juncture to pause and summarize Savarkar's project of defining the Hindu Self in opposition to the non-self. The primary non-self in his case was Islam and its followers. There were elements in Islam that Savarkar admired and perceived as missing in the Hindu character. Notions of a militant church, community spirit and fierce religiosity were desirable attributes and had to be incorporated and absorbed within the Hindu Self. The Prophet had to be admired because he held the Holy Qur'an in one hand and a sword in the other. Also, Islam had at one time replaced and invigorated a decaying civilization and brought new light to millions of people.

At the same time, Savarkar had to ensure that the difference between the Self and the non-self was not obliterated. The Hindu Self had to maintain its identity and distinctiveness and at the same time be equal to the non-self in several important ways. This entailed a definition of the non-self by Savarkar. In order to distance the Hindu Self sufficiently from the Islamic non-self this was imperative. Savarkar's account of the founding and spread of Islam, as we have seen, accomplished this admirably. That this process of defining and distancing the Self from the non-self possibly led to a caricaturing of the non-self is to be understood in the context of competing faiths fighting over doctrinal supremacy, moral and ethical exclusivity and political power.

The next logical step for Savarkar in completing the process of distancing and defining the Hindu Self from the Islamic non-self would be to trace the encounter of the Self and the non-self in India. Savarkar was acutely aware of the gulf that invariably lay between the scriptural and doctrinal basis of any religion and its actual practice. He would have to contend with this factor, as we shall see in Section IV, in the case of defining Hindutva as opposed to Hinduism. Islam too presented him with similar difficulties. He would summarily brush aside such contradictions between doctrine and practice in favour of the supremacy of practice.

In 1927, Savarkar wrote a play called *Sangeet Uhshraap*.[32] It was staged in April of the same year and banned two months later, in June. Untouchability among the Hindus, the decadence prevalent among upper-caste Hindus, untouchability leading to conversion to Islam, the limitations of Brahminical Hinduism and the Muslim agenda in India figure prominently as themes in the play.

In Act IV, Scene 3, Subedaar Bangash Khan is seen talking to himself. The theme is, predictably, the mission of Islam in India. In the nuances of this monologue and the subsequent dialogues between Bangash Khan and Maulvi Zafar Ali insights are gained on Savarkar's definition of Islam:

> Bangash Khan: The more I abduct Hindu girls and include them in my zenana, the more my respect among Muslims enhances. Maulvi Zafar Ali has shown that enjoyment of temporal pleasures clears the way to otherworldly benefits. I have corrupted so many Hindu girls and made them my mistresses that hundreds of Muslims consider me a true missionary and preacher of Islam; this is because I have produced progeny through

> these women who are Muslims ... He [Maulvi Zafar Ali] has given us a fine tool: Fulfillment of lust through faith and fulfillment of faith through lust. What have we got to do with what is said in the Qur'an? Enjoy the girls of the kaafirs, corrupt them, this mantra of Zafar Ali is my Qur'an.[33]

Note the nuances of Savarkar's argument articulated through the speech of Bangash Khan: Muslims are sensuous, lascivious, immoral, unethical and impious.

At this point, Maulvi Zafar Ali enters, accompanied by Mullaji, a pious Muslim cleric, and elaborates on what Savarkar, his theatrical creator, considers as the Muslim agenda in India:

> Zafar Ali: We have become rulers by smashing the throne of the Hindus. We have enslaved the kshatriyas and razed to dust their conventions. Muhammad Gaznavi and Muhammad Gori have smashed idols from Hindu temples and buried them under the steps of mosques. Lakhs of Hindus have been converted through the force of the sword. Their girls have been made our slaves. That is why the destruction of Hindu customs, conventions, beliefs, people, wealth and morale is our duty and essential to the spread and dissemination of Islam. We must increase our numbers also through encouraging their suicidal superstitions and outdated conventions.[34]

Desecration of Hindu temples, conversions by 'force or fraud', corrupting of Hindu girls and the overall destruction of Hinduism—these themes were to forever remain Savarkar's shorthand symbols for characterizing Islam.

Mullaji, till now a silent spectator to the conversation between Bangash Khan and Zafar Ali, interjects and says that this way of disseminating the teachings of the Qur'an was to bring disgrace to it.[35] The Qur'an, he says, teaches generosity. Even the Hindus have had lofty metaphysics and famous saints and seers. If the message of the Qur'an is to be spread, it should be done through love, not through realpolitik, not by raping girls and certainly not with the help of the force of the sword. A faith that spreads, Mullaji argues, through such means is not a divine faith but a demonic faith. The subedaar asks Mullaji to shut up. He says that Zafar Ali and he had been following the path shown by thousands of maulvis and martyrs of faith.

From this last speech, it is evident that the tension within Savarkar's thought about the place of the normative and the practical remains irresoluble. If anything at all, as we shall see in pages that follow, the normative often came in the way of Savarkar achieving his more immediate political goals. Most significantly, Savarkar would have to contend with Hinduism as a doctrinally plural and ritualistically rich faith confronting his unified, monochromatic and politically directed notion of Hindutva.

Interestingly, *Sangeet Uhshraap* belongs to the phase of Savarkar's other mature works, including *Hindutva*, *Hindu-Pad-Padashahi*, *Uttarkriya*, and *Sanyastha Khadga*. All these were written in Ratnagiri, between 1921 and 1937. After his release in 1921 from prison in the Andamans, Savarkar was confined till January 1924 in Ratnagiri jail. He was then released conditionally but could not step out of the district limits of Ratnagiri or indulge in any form of political activity without the permission of the British government. His confinement to Ratnagiri ended in 1937. Common to these texts, as with the more popularly known works like *Kala Pani* (1937)[36] and *How Does It Concern Me, or the Mopla Carnage* (1924),[37] is a stridency regarding the place of Muslims in India. Without exception, these are political texts, a demonstration of the most extreme political rhetoric. Free to express his political views more openly, Savarkar engaged in splenetic outbursts against Muslims, Congressmen and Gandhi—a direct reaction to the politics of that period.

In *Hindutva*,[38] Savarkar quoted Ramdas, Shivaji's guru and mentor, who characterized Muslims as those who hated Hindusthan and had sinned against the Hindu God, and so were defilers of religion. Cited is Govindrao Kale's letter to Nana Fadnavis that speaks about the Muslims preventing Hindus from wearing the sacred thread. A letter written by the people of Savnoor district to Shivaji is mentioned in which the villagers speak of atrocities committed by Muslims against women and children as well as the slaughter of cows by them.

Writing the history of the Hindu Empire of Maharashtra in *Hindu-Pad-Padashahi*, Savarkar recruited God on the side of the image worshippers rather than on the side of the image breakers.[39] Once Maratha supremacy was established, Savarkar asserted, the 'blustering Maulanas and Maulvis' had to admit that the image worshippers with their beardless chins had defeated their central proposition: That the conquering spree of Islam was a proof of God siding with the Muslim faith.[40] The intemperance and violence of Savarkar's rhetoric need to be read in the original, only if it serves to understand the vocabulary of current votaries of Hindutva:

> The temple towered high above the mosque. The crescent waned and gasped for its life and the sun rose heating the proud and splendid summits of Hinduism in molten gold ... Aurangzeb had snorted out 'Rats', the rats bearded the lion in his own den and pulled out his claws and teeth one by one; the cows killed the butcher; even as our Guru Govind foretold, the hawks were hacked to pieces by the sparrows.[41]

In other words, the 'effete' Hindus had acquired the requisite machismo to take on Islam.

Savarkar's rhetoric against Muslims attained an all-time high in the 1930s and early 1940s, especially as he increasingly reacted to the matching stridency and vitriol generated by Jinnah and Muslim League politics. Savarkar questioned the fidelity of Muslims towards India. This, he argued, was a direct consequence of their fanatical religion, whose holy land lay outside the territorial limits of India.[42] They still cherished the dream of re-establishing Muslim rule in India. He constantly harped on the theme of Muslims being anti-Hindu, anti-Indian and harbouring pan-Islamic ambitions. The sole purpose of Muslim League politics was to humiliate the Hindus and establish Muslim domination.[43] From the presidential chair of the Hindu Mahasabha's annual session held at Ahmedabad in 1937, Savarkar clearly stated that 'there are two antagonistic nations living side by side in India ...'.[44] 'Nation' here did not have the gloss that Jinnah's two-nation theory would acquire after 1940. It referred merely to racial types.

It was not adequate, argued Savarkar, to label the Muslim League communal: The whole Muslim community was communal.[45] Why? Their theology and theocratic politics divided the world into two categories: Muslim land and enemy land. All lands inhabited by non-Muslims were enemy lands and no good Muslim could bear allegiance to such a land till it was conquered and the people there converted to Islam. Further, the Hindus were seen as the most damned by Muslims. This was because, unlike the Christians and the Jews, Hindus were not 'kitabis', people of the book. Hindusthan was for the Muslims *Dar-ul-Harb,* enemy land, not *Dar-ul-Islam,* the land of the faithful.

III

Despite Savarkar's regular barbs against Muslim theocratic politics, religion formed the very basis of politics for Savarkar. The epigraph of Savarkar's essay on the First War of Independence of 1857[46] is taken from Swami Ramdas. It says: 'Die for the sake of dharma, and while dieing kill all; in killing is your victory, the establishment of your own rule.'[47] Savarkar considers 1857 to be a political revolution on the lines of what happened in Mazzini's Italy, but the essence of which was the establishment and reinstatement of swadharma or 'own religion', and swarajya or self-rule. The English had attacked both religion and freedom and these had to be retrieved and rescued from alien hands.

What was the connection between swadharma and swarajya? The ancients believed, said Savarkar, that the two were inseparable. Mazzini, he pointed out, too held the same view, that heaven and earth were two ends of the same thing and could not be dissociated.[48] The dream of political independence was not different from the conception of swarajya but the latter went further; in fact, 'Swarajya is worthless without Swadharma and Swadharma is powerless without Swarajya'.[49] The sword of swarajya must always be ready to defend swadharma. In ancient times, revolutions always took a religious turn and went hand in hand with religion and religious sanction. Never mind the ancients, even Mazzini said the same.[50]

Continuing the religious vein of his argument, Savarkar asserted: All true faiths condemn dependence. Wherever there is God, there can be no loss of independence and slavery; wherever God does not reside, there is no religion and righteousness there. Loss of independence is a breach of God's will. That is the reason why there is special sanction for 'piercing the throat of this vile demon'[51] of dependence. The English, who have subjugated Hindus and Muslims alike, were guilty of impiety. To gain independence from them was, therefore, the primary duty of religion.

Inhabiting a world polarized by categories of friend and foe, Savarkar now came to look upon Muslims as natural allies against the English. Mazzini had written in *On Nationality*: 'Whichever people, by its superiority of strength, and by its geographical position, can do us injury, is our natural enemy; whichever cannot do us injury, but can by the amount of its force and by its position injure our enemy, is our natural ally.'[52] Savarkar agreed with this completely. The English were guilty of the very sins that were once attributed to the Muslims. They tried to convert Hindus to Christianity, they had come to loot and plunder the wealth of India because materialism was more important to them than Jesus, they interfered with Hindu practices under the guise of reform and abused Hindu gods and goddesses. Muslims too had to bear abuses being heaped on the Prophet.

The English were the 'natural enemy'. The Hindus and Muslims fought against this common foe 'hand in hand, shoulder to shoulder in 1857'.[53] Muslim maulvis were recruited by the leaders of 1857 to sow the seeds of revolution. They preached 'political jihad'.[54] The dharmagurus, religious preachers of Hindus and Muslims waged jihad against the English rule. Maulvi Ahmedshah, Vazir Ali and Nakhi Khan were praised in the same breath as Nana Saheb. They were 'deshbhakta', patriots. The Hindu and Muslim races showed complete friendship during 1857.

Five days of battle to capture Delhi brought an end to the war between the Hindus and the Muslims that had begun with the attacks of Muhammad Ghazni. 'It was during these days,' exults Savarkar, 'that the sense of otherness and the feelings of victor-vanquished vanished and there appeared a feeling of mutual friendship.'[55] Shivaji, Rana Pratap, Chhatrasaal and Guru Govindsingh had freed Hindus from the Muslim yoke, and now Mother

India was acknowledging Hindus and Muslims as blood brothers.[56] This was the spirit that made Hindus and Muslims rebel and grow impatient to end foreign rule in India. Differences of faith were forgotten and did not come in the way of national unity in 1857.

After the sense of otherness vanished and the Hindu Self and the Muslim non-self became blood brothers, they unleashed an unprecedented degree of violence against their English adversaries. This is not to suggest that the English were blameless. Rather, the violence and its celebration by Savarkar points to the absence in his thought of an alternative moral and normative framework. He remained a prisoner of the view that holds 'might is right' as the decisive category in politics, and the axiom 'eye for an eye, tooth for a tooth' to be the only way to correct instances of slight, injury or persecution.

*

The Partition riots and the violence between Hindus and Muslims in independent India have often affected women and children the most. More recently, there was a degree of callousness and insouciance on all sides regarding the violence meted out to women and children during the riots in Gujarat between February and April 2002. This narrative will, therefore, confine itself to Savarkar's justification of violence against women and children in his essay on 1857. His spiritual children or manas putras in the Sangh Parivar have often claimed monopoly over morality and rectitude. However, citing examples from Savarkar's celebration of such violence would question this moral certitude. It would also suggest that Savarkar transformed Hindutva into the very image of the Islam he defined and found so intolerably objectionable.

A few examples from Savarkar's 'The First War of Independence of 1857' would suffice to illustrate these points. In Meerut, the rebels made rivers of blood of the English flow. Several women and children died after their houses were set on fire. Savarkar notes that the more English blood split, the more the rebels began to rejoice loudly.[57] In Delhi, Jenning, his young daughter and a lady guest of theirs were killed. Bahadurshah Zafar had given refuge to a few Englishmen and women but they were soon eliminated. If some woman or child pleaded for mercy, the vengeful sword of the men leading the revolution decapitated the pleading head.[58]

In Allahabad, most English children were in the fort and were killed.[59] Savarkar describes this without emotion. A few pages later, he justifies the killings on the ground that they were for the sake of swadharma and swarajya. It was a consequence of a hundred years of slavery. It was natural to retaliate and take revenge. The word Savarkar uses is 'pratishodh'. In Kanpur, Colonel Evert's wife was told that she was being spared because she was a woman. 'What woman! Isn't she a white woman? If so, cut her to pieces,' shouted a rebel. Mrs Evert was killed.

Englishmen, women and children were put on boats in Kanpur and asked to leave. This is what happened when they were in the Ganga:

> In the meantime, the boats started burning. English men, women and children started leaping in the Ganga.

> Some started swimming, some drowned, some started burning and all of them, sooner or later, were killed by bullets. Pieces of flesh, decapitated heads, strands of hair, disembodied hands, broken legs, a flood of blood. The Ganga turned red ... this is how the anniversary of Plassey was celebrated![60]

Savarkar's reference to 'celebrating' the anniversary of Plassey in this manner is noteworthy.

There is still more to come. Here is Savarkar's unemotional account of what happened in Bibigarh, in Kanpur. The scene is one where the prison guards refuse to massacre the English. Begum Saheb, the chief officer of Bibigarh, which is under rebel control, sends a message to the butcher's colony in Kanpur:

> In a short while, the butchers entered Bibigarh with naked swords and sharp knives in the evening and emerged out of it late in the night. Between their entering and coming out, a sea of white blood spread all over. As soon as they entered with their swords and knives, they butchered one hundred and fifty women and children. A pool of blood collected there and body parts floated in it. While going in, the butchers walked on the ground and while coming out they had to journey through blood.[61]

And then, this is what happened next morning:

> As soon as it was morning, these poor creatures [those who were half-dead or dying] were dragged out and were pushed into a nearby well. Two children got out from under the weight of bodies and started running

> around the edge of the well. But they were pushed back into the well and fell over the dead.[62]

Savarkar comments that the account accumulated between the two races had been squared in this manner.

Something similar happened in Jhansi prison. Sixty Englishmen, women and children were massacred. This is how Savarkar describes it:

> Women had little children in their laps and these children were clinging on to their mothers. Those women, infants and older children who were clinging on to their mothers were guilty of being white and were decapitated with a black sword.[63]

Savarkar's reaction: This was how the great injustice of Jhansi was avenged.

This was not a mere massacre, he says, but a holy, ritualistic sacrifice, a 'bali'. At one point, when the English caught the rebellious soldiers, and before they were hanged, the English asked them why they had killed their women and children. The soldiers replied: 'Sir, does anyone leave behind the litter of a snake after killing the snake?'[64]

The story doesn't end here. A justification of revenge, retaliation and retribution was carefully built into Savarkar's retelling of 1857. A massacre, he says, is a terrible thing. It happens, however, because humankind has failed to approximate the lofty ideals of natural justice, peace, parity and universal brotherhood.[65] In this day and age, asatya, untruth, rules over satya, truth. We can only wait for an era to dawn when truth will rule every heart. If someone in such an era were to spill blood or even utter the word pratishodh or revenge, he/she would automatically be considered vile, wretched and lowly. Acts of revenge in a society where ahimsa, non-violence, and justice rule would be considered sinful.

Savarkar regretted that such a divine epoch was far from being realized. Words like revolt, revolution, rebellion and revenge, therefore, were legitimate in order to remove injustice and bring about parity and justice.[66] Revolt, bloodshed and revenge were at once the instruments of injustice and of bringing about natural justice. That is why Shivaji's claws were sacred, that is the reason Brutus's dagger was sacred and that is why the bloodshed of Italy's revolution was without blemish. Fear keeps a check on injustice. 'For every Hiranyakashyapu,' Savarkar quips, 'a Narasimha is essential; every Duhshasana requires a Bheema.'[67]

Revenge, therefore, was the establishment of natural law and justice. From this axiom, Savarkar derived a principle of nationalism. He claimed that wherever injustice increased and nations went up in flames, wherever nationalist wars were fought, in such places revenge for injustices that the nation suffered were taken by killing the perpetrators of injustice of another nation.[68]

This was not only part and parcel of Savarkar's theory of nationalism but also his lifelong project to make Hindus more manly. In the Madura session of the Hindu Mahasabha in 1940, Savarkar gave a clear exposition of his cherished goal:

> It is in this spirit that I want all Hindus to get themselves re-animated and re-born into a martial race. Manu and Shri Krishna are our law givers and Shri Rama the

> Commander of our forces. Let us re-learn the manly lessons they taught us and our Hindu Nation shall prove again as unconquerable and conquering a race as we proved once when they led us: conquering those who dared to be aggressive against us and refraining ourselves, not out of weakness but out of magnanimity, from any unjustifiable designs of aggression against the unoffending.[69]

The Hindus were a martial race, says Savarkar, with a history of great men who showed the path of manliness in the face of aggression. He admitted that there was a parallel tradition of forgiveness and non-aggression that was born out of Hindu superiority and magnanimity.

The above words justifying the Hindu martial strain were an outcome of Savarkar's denunciation of Gandhi and his philosophy of ahimsa, non-violence. Savarkar calls it 'the monomaniacal principle of absolute non-violence'.[70] Absolute non-violence in the face of incorrigible aggression was immoral. It was not 'an outcome of any saintliness but of insanity'.[71] Even the Jains and the Buddhists had made exceptions to their philosophy of ahimsa.

Ahimsa was the other non-self (apart from Islam) that Savarkar's Hindu Self had to contend with. It was the only impediment in the completion of Savarkar's definition of a martial, forward-thrusting, unforgiving and aggressive Hindu Self. He had to reconcile with and neutralize the challenge posed by this formidable non-self, especially because ahimsa was rooted in the very Hindu civilization, which Savarkar privileged and celebrated.

The very embodiment of 'the mealy-mouthed formulas of Ahimsa and spiritual brotherhood'[72] was the Buddha.

Before launching his diatribe against the Buddha's philosophy, Savarkar played safe by paying a qualified tribute to the Enlightened One. He spoke of 'our love, admiration and respect for the Buddha—the Dharma—the Sangha'.[73] They belong to the Hindu people. Their glories and failures are in equal measure 'ours'.

Buddhism's glories, however, belonged to a world far removed from Savarkar's matter-of-fact world.[74] Here were found feet of clay and trishna or thirst so powerful and real they could not be quenched by the promise of nirvana. It was a world where steel could be easily sharpened. When the Huns and the Shakas poured into India 'like volcanic torrents', the Indians—in this passage Savarkar uses the term 'Indians' as a synonym for Hindus—realized that while they were superior to the hordes of barbarians invading India in language, religion, philosophy and mercy, the invaders were superior in 'Fire and Sword'.[75] Buddhist logic was incapable of meeting this challenge, 'this strange Bible of Fire and Steel'.[76] The leaders of thought and action in India had to rekindle the sacrificial fire of the Vedas, to sharpen the steel of war at the altar of Kali so that 'the Mahakal—the "Spirit of Time" [could] be appeased'.[77]

National and racial distinctions in the world made men brutal. Savarkar was convinced that exchange of sword for rosary could not subdue animal passions, political ambitions or individual aggrandizement. Any talk, therefore, of international brotherhood and man's common humanity was utopian in the extreme. The dualism of fire and sword could not be abandoned as long as 'the whole world was red in tooth and claw'.[78] The solution was a state backed by a religion, a 'church' as he puts it, which was intensely national. Only that could revive India's ability to resist sin, crime and aggression.[79] Ahimsa and universalism had weakened these institutions and their ability to withstand external assaults on the nation, religion and race.

Savarkar wrote two plays centred around themes connected with the life of the Buddha. *Bodhivriksha*[80] remained incomplete. The second play, *Sanyastha Khadga (The Renunciate Sword)* is a most lucid exposition of Savarkar's rejection of ahimsa and advocacy of violence. These plays have to be read also as thinly veiled attacks on the Mahatma and his philosophical system.

A substantial part of *Sanyastha Khadga* is devoted to debates between Vikram Singh, the commander-in-chief of the Shakya kingdom, and the Buddha. To begin with, Vikram is a karmayogi who does not believe in renouncing the world. He believes in living in the world and developing the attitudes of a renunciate. The Buddha talks of the middle path and the need to embrace sanyas, renunciation. This, in turn, entails a rejection of kamini or women, krishi or agriculture, and khadga or arms. Vikram says that all these rejections are harmful for society and for the nation, more so the rejection of arms. Vikram considers an excessive preoccupation with ahimsa as self-destructive. Destruction of the self is a form of himsa, violence.[81] In the end, extreme ahimsa gets transformed into extreme violence.

Vikram sees the end result of renunciation and ahimsa as enslavement in the hands of other nations. Ahimsa weakens because an evil enemy usually fails to recognize forgiveness and mercy. He does not see an end to the primacy of arms and of war; for him 'might is right' remains a cardinal principle. The Buddha retorts that the only weapon that a sanyasi has is mercy. Vikram counters him by saying that one who does not have the ability to punish cannot forgive. Without strength, forgiveness is capitulation. Such forgiveness is the characteristic of a refugee. The Buddha concedes that it is all right to strike and finish an aggressor and put an end to violence as long as a householder and not a sanyasi does this.

Despite warning the Buddha of the consequences of ahimsa and the giving up of warfare, Vikram joins the Buddha and becomes a renunciate himself. Some years later, the Shakya kingdom is attacked. Only Vikram can save them from being invaded. There is a final showdown in the play between him and the Buddha. At the end of this confrontation, Vikram gives up being a renunciatc and goes out to fight a war.

Vikram's arguments echo Savarkar's own sentiments about ahimsa and the pre-eminent position he grants to violence in the process of nation building.

This is how Vikram's argument proceeds: Abandoning arms is against public good. The strength of the arms of the wicked subdues virtue and the semblance of all dharma, righteousness. Only power, authority and the strength of arms can bring about genuine ahimsa. To ignore the defence of a nation is to commit a sin. The Buddha wants to eliminate evil from the very roots of human character—a more durable solution. Vikram rejects this as impractical. In the closing scenes of the play, Vikram saves the Buddha from being murdered. Only the sword can save the sage, Vikram says.[82]

The play ends with the appearance of an embodied Dharma. Vikram gives a very Krishna-like discourse. He utters a prophecy about the weakening of India and it being under threat from foreigners. To overcome this, he prescribes karmayoga.

Having confronted the non-violent non-self, Savarkar's next step was to define his conception of a Hindu Rashtra that was strong in fire and sword.

IV

Giuseppe Mazzini was an unlikely prophet of Indian nationalism. He believed in the rights and dignity of man, in the law of progress and the joint destiny of humanity. He was a passionate humanitarian liberal.[83] While he argued in favour of nationality and patriotism, his ideals were to be systematically distorted towards national self-glorification and moral superiority of particular peoples and races.[84] All Indian nationalists from Surendranath Banerjea to Bipin Chandra Pal and from Savarkar to Gandhi were deeply influenced by Mazzini's political philosophy.

The idea of national liberty was central to Mazzini's thought. For him, liberty and the individual were sacred. He, however, sought to replace individualism with the idea of the epoch of the peoples finding their natural manifestation in the collective life of nationality. The primary prerequisites of nationality were the acknowledgement of being indigenous within a state and the principle of unity. Without unity, Mazzini asserted, there was no true nation, no real strength and no genuine ability to fight one's powerful enemies. This unity was of free men and women who were equals, but it also entailed a harmony between heaven and earth, between religion and politics. While there was room for respect for religious beliefs of other 'nations', it was imperative that any future political organization of the nation should ensure unity of religious belief.

Nationality demanded a name. It was to be driven by a desire to make the country powerful, respected, free and happy. Once independence, unity and liberty were achieved, the sanctity of the principle of nationality could be ensured. Nationality was no artificial or juridical construct for Mazzini. It was the binding together of people through the common bonds of language, traditions, ethnicity, geography and a deeper sense of community. The watchword of nationality was duty as contrasted with the individualist's credo of rights. Duty towards others and towards society was paramount and gave meaning to true liberty. Liberty without equality was empty legalism.

A nation was, therefore, not a mere aggregate of individuals. Mazzini felt that the idea of nationality required a positive affirmation to an idea of collectivity and to a larger purpose than the mere enhancement of individual liberty. In a nation, people 'speak the same language, they bear about them the impress of consanguinity, they kneel beside the same tombs, they glory in the same tradition; and they demand to associate freely, without obstacles, without foreign domination, in order to elaborate and express their idea; to contribute their stone also to the great pyramid of history'.[85] Self-determination, it followed, was a rightful and irresistible idea.

Mazzini was not unaware that nascent nationalities could be hostile to each other and could tend to regard their own claims as ends in themselves.[86] This was to be brushed aside in favour of the larger cause of establishing the sovereignty of the people. To battle for freedom and justice was to work for a holy cause. Revolt was sacred. When the chance of re-enthroning right, justice and security through peaceful means disappeared, brutal physical force stood between mankind and progress. Only 'canceling the life of the wicked' can save the life of the good and the brave.[87]

In a tract titled *Instructions for the Members of Young Italy,* written for a secret society of the same name he had founded, Mazzini writes about guerilla insurrection as the true method of warfare for all nations aspiring to become independent of foreign rule. Such insurrection also helps to form the military character of the people and consecrates every inch of the native soil by the meaning of some warlike deed. In another tract titled *Rules for the Conduct of Guerrilla Bands,* Mazzini explains guerilla warfare as an instrument that opens a field of activity for every local capacity. It forces the enemy into a mode of battle he is unaccustomed to. It is an invincible and indestructible method because it saves the guerillas from great defeats and it has the advantage of not being restricted to a definite and fixed set of operations.

Savarkar often spoke of Shivaji and Mazzini in the same breath. In his account of 1857, Savarkar refers to Mazzini's commentary on Carlyle's book on the French Revolution and says that the 'famous philosopher and patriot Mazzini'[88] had emphasized the need for every revolution to have at its foundation some essence. Savarkar never tires of quoting Mazzini. In *Hindu-Pad-Padashahi,* comparisons are drawn between the guerilla tactics of Shivaji and that of Mazzini.[89] Such was the influence of Mazzini, that in 1906, Savarkar compiled a 300-page text on him, later known as *Mazzini Charitra.* This was a translation of selected writings of Mazzini with Savarkar's twenty-five-page introduction.

The introduction to *Mazzini Charitra* has themes that fascinated Savarkar during his days as a revolutionary freedom fighter. He writes approvingly of Mazzini's tactics of organizing secret societies and the desirability of guerilla warfare. Mazzini's views on nationality, however, find the greatest resonance with Savarkar. In an essay titled 'Joseph Mazzini: Autobiography and Politics',[90] Savarkar recalls his discovery of Mazzini's work in the India House Library in London and his attempt to translate the Italian patriot's writings into Marathi. Even this chapter alludes to the impact Mazzini's views on nationality had on Savarkar, for he chooses certain significant passages from his own book to illustrate the path shown by Mazzini to nations fighting for freedom from foreign rule.

Love the soil of your motherland; the land where your ancestors sleep is your motherland; the land where the object of your love first uttered the word 'love', that is your motherland. Your land is your home because God has granted it to you. Your country is your pride, your grandeur and the very symbol of your fame. Give your country your blood and thought. Keep it united and prevent it from being fragmented. The Almighty has demarcated the boundaries and limits of your country with his own fingers.[91] These are recurrent themes in Mazzini's thought that Savarkar identified with and made the guiding principles of his own brand of nationalism.

*

Savarkar's speeches as president of the Hindu Mahasabha after 1937 are the clearest exposition of his vision of a Hindu Rashtra. There is a great deal of rhetoric in these public utterances in favour of 'an Indian State in which all citizens irrespective of caste and creed, race and religion are treated all alike on the principle of one man one vote'.[92] The very next sentence talks about the Hindus being the overwhelming majority in India. Savarkar begins his 1937 address at Ahmedabad by clearly stating that as far as the Hindus were concerned, there could be no distinction or tension between their communal and national duties, which, in turn, are identifiable with the best interests of Hindusthan as a whole.[93]

Delineating the future shape of the Indian Nation, Savarkar goes on to say that Hindus were the 'bedrock on which an Indian independent state could be built'.[94] The consolidation and the independence of the Hindu nation was, therefore, another name for the independence of the Indian nation as a whole. In other words, India's independence was inextricably linked to 'the independence of our people, our race, our nation'.[95] Hindus had to be 'masters in our own house'[96] and that was the essence of political independence for India as well.

The mastery of one's own house for Savarkar meant ensuring the primacy of the religion, race and cultural identity of the Hindus. Merely winning geographical independence, that is, independence of the Indian territory and the state, was not good enough.[97] Independent India must ensure and protect the Hindutva of the Hindus.

In defining Hindutva, Savarkar had to first distance the terms 'Hindu' and 'Hindutva' from the commonly accepted cognate 'Hinduism'. This was the defining mission of his life. Many years after he wrote his seminal work, *Hindutva,* Savarkar continued to emphasize the sharp distinction between 'Hindutva' and 'Hinduism' at every given opportunity. Addressing the Hindu Mahasabha session in 1937, he says:

> [T]he concept of the term 'Hindutva'—Hinduness—is more comprehensive than the word 'Hinduism'. It was to draw a pointed attention to this distinction that I had coined the words 'Hindutva', 'Pan Hindu' and 'Hindudom' when I framed the definition of the word 'Hindu'. Hinduism concerns with the religious system of the Hindus, their theology and dogma.[98]

Theology and dogma were thus to be left entirely to individual or group conscience and belief.

Writing years after the publication of *Hindutva,* Savarkar was emphatic that Hindutva was not a turban worn in a particular style, nor was it to be located in the pages of the *Brahmasutra,* or in the symbolism of a priest's tuft of hair, and least of all in cow piss, gomutra. Hindutva, he wrote, is the life of a great race.[99] His seed text, *Hindutva,* began with this very premise.

Mazzini had asserted that a nationality needed a name. On the fifth line on page 1 of *Hindutva,* Savarkar made an unequivocal statement: 'Hindus we are and love to remain so!'[100] Having thus got nomenclature out of the way, Savarkar quickly moved on to defining Hindutva as distinct from Hinduism. Hindutva was not a word, he asserted, but a history. It was not a sliver of history but history in full. Hinduism, in contrast, was only a derivative, a fraction, and a part of Hindutva.[101] Without defining Hindutva, Hinduism was bound to remain unintelligible. Hindutva meant being primarily unconcerned about religious dogma or theocratic rules or a creed.

The gulf between Hindutva and Hinduism widened as Savarkar proceeded in his definition of Hindutva. Not only was Hinduism a derivative, it was also a word that was an 'alien growth'.[102] It was a 'new-fangled term' which ought not to be allowed to cloud the thoughts of Hindus. In fact, there was no axiomatic relationship between being a Hindu and belief in the entity called 'Hinduism'.[103] In fact, people baulked from owning up they were Hindus because of the dogmas and religious practices associated with Hinduism. Savarkar categorically stated that there was no connection between being a true Hindu and, say, believing in the authority of the Vedas.

Hindutva, in sharp contrast, was a composite term that embraced 'all departments of thought and activity of the whole *Being* of our Hindu race'.[104] But in order to fully grasp the significance of Hindutva, it was important to understand the essential meaning of the word 'Hindu'. In this enterprise, Savarkar posed himself two questions:

'What is a Hindu?' and 'Who is a Hindu?' Sandwiched between the two questions was the explanation of the essential implications of Hindutva.

Savarkar's responded to the question 'What is a Hindu?' by turning to the 'glimmering twilight of history'.[105] The Aryans arrived and spread themselves out along the seven rivers, the Sapta Sindhus. They gave the land where they settled and themselves a local name, Sapta Sindhu. The Prakrit languages transformed the 'S' into 'H' and so Sapta Sindhu became Hapta Hindu. To illustrate this, Savarkar marshalled evidence from the Avesta and the *Bhavishya Purana.* It was, therefore, beyond doubt that Sapta Sindhu was the 'first and almost the cradle name chosen by the patriarchs of our race'[106] to designate a nation and a people.

The Aryans began to incorporate different people into their culture, forming new identities and attachments. These new entities were so potent that the old names and generalizations were overshadowed and forgotten. Despite names like Aryavarta, Bharatvarsha or Bharatkhanda gaining currency, the world knew the inhabitants of this land as 'Hindus' and the land itself as 'Hindusthan'. What remained, therefore, was the conception of a national and cultural unity. To prove that the Sindhus had after all founded a nation and a country, at this juncture, becomes crucial to Savarkar's enterprise of positing an overarching idea of Hindutva.

Proof of founding a nation and a country with defined geographical boundaries was to be found in the pages of the epics. A nation and a country was founded when 'the valorous Prince of Ayodhya made a triumphant entry in Ceylon and actually brought the whole land from the Himalayas to the Seas under one sovereign sway'.[107] It was then the Prince of Ayodhya who established the Hindu nation:

> The day when the Horse of Victory returned to Ayodhya unchallenged and unchallengeable, the great white Umbrella of Sovereignty was unfurled over that Imperial throne of Ramachandra, the brave, Ramachandra the good, and a loving allegiance to him was sworn, not only by the Princes of the Aryan blood but Hanuman, Sugriva, Bibhishana from the south—that day was the real birthday of our Hindu people.[108]

It was a national day because the Aryans and the non-Aryans knitted themselves together as a people. The very idea of a nation posits a common mission, a common banner and a common cause. In other words, unity was essential to the manufacture of a nation. Mazzini had said so, and Savarkar agreed without reservations.

This notion of nation and nationality, however, was too tentative. The Hindu Self at this juncture came into direct conflict with a series of non-selves, a process that helped in defining the nation. Buddhism, while espousing non-violence and universalism, opened Hindusthan to foreign aggression. It also destroyed an institution that helped define nationality. This was the varna system, the fourfold classification of castes based on division of labour. The varna system distinguished 'us' from foreigners. This system was useful once but did not serve Savarkar's political agenda of defining Hindutva and bringing about unity among the Hindus. Hence, varna as a marker of identity was found to be too exclusive and restrictive and dropped as a defining category.

Next, Savarkar returned to the idea of territoriality and built another set of scaffolding around it. The most ancient name of our country, he maintained, was Sapta Sindhu or Sindhu. The river, Sindhu or Indus, after which the land and people derived their names, was the 'vital spinal cord that connects the remotest past to the remotest future'.[109] But this did not take him far in demarcating the national boundaries of Hindusthan. The argument, at this point, was given a crucial twist:

> The word Sindhu in Sanskrit does not only mean the Indus but also the Sea—which girdles the southern peninsula—so that this one word Sindhu points out almost all frontiers of the land at a single stroke.[110]

The land that lay between Sindhu, the river, and Sindhu, another name for the seas that surround peninsular India, was 'our whole Motherland'.[111] It was a cohesive geographical unit, not merely a piece of land but a nation. What made it a nation was also the idea of cultural unity.

This notion of cultural unity had the potential of opening a can of worms for Savarkar. While the cultural superiority of the Aryans was regularly flaunted, there was little to conclusively make a case for cultural unity. Savarkar deftly sidestepped the issue, claimed the authority of the Vedas and broadened the definition of 'Arya' to include non-Aryans as well. The word 'Arya', therefore, included all those people 'who had been integrated as parts integral in the nation and people that flourished on this our side of the Indus whether Vaidik or Avaidik, Bramhana or Chandal, and owning and claiming to have inherited a common culture, common blood, common country and common polity'.[112] The only category that stood outside the pale of this perfect unity postulated by Savarkar were the mlechchhas, foreigners nationally and racially.

What distinguished this ideally unified world of the Hindus, then, was the presence of the foreigner as the non-self. In turn, the varna system created the distinction between Hindus and mlechchhas. As long as the varna system remained in place as a marker of identity and nationality, the idea of a perfectly unified Hindu nationality would invariably be susceptible to dissidence. Caste had once served a useful purpose in demarcating the indigenous from the alien. But it had outlived its usefulness as a facilitator of nationality. Rhetorically, Savarkar puts the question as to whether all Sindhus/ Hindus would become foreigners if the caste system ceased to exist or failed to serve its purpose. He says:

> The Sanyasis, the Aryasamajis, the Sikhs and many others do not recognize the system of four castes and yet are they foreigners? God forbid! They are ours by blood, by race, by country, by God. 'Its name is Bharat and the people are Bharati' is a definition ten times better because truer than that. We Hindus[113] are all one and a nation, because chiefly of our common blood—; 'Bharati Santati'.

The only thing that threatened this idyllic unity and peace, therefore, was the foreigner.

Conflict with the Mlechchhas—Arabs, Turks, Persians, Tartars, Pathans, Baluchis, Mughals—defined Hindu identity and constituted the Hindus as a nation. The Hindus fought under the banner of Hindutva and transcended the particularities of caste and creed. Savarkar argued that all castes, creeds and denominations 'suffered as Hindus and triumphed as Hindus'.[114] All peoples and races, he went on to add, from Attock to Cuttack were transformed into a single Being. Hindutva—Hinduness—permeated the whole body politic and made the Nairs of Malabar weep over the sufferings of the Brahmins of Kashmir.

Having broadly defined what is a Hindu in territorial and cultural terms, and having traced the development of Hindu identity and nationality, Savarkar embarked on the crucial task of formulating the implications of Hindutva. The first essential of Hindutva was a geographical one. Hindusthan was the land of the Hindus—and a Hindu was 'primarily a citizen either in himself or through his forefathers of "Hindusthan" and claims the land as his motherland'.[115] By implication, therefore, a Muslim resident of India would also be entitled to call himself a Hindu. Savarkar was quick to reject this claim. He qualified his stand saying, maybe in some future day and age when all 'isms' cease to exist and when cultural and religious bigotry is a thing of the past, the 'word Hindu may come to indicate a citizen of Hindusthan and nothing else'.[116]

Inhabiting the territory designated as Hindusthan was, however, not sufficient to either be a Hindu or to participate in the continuum called Hindutva. It was imperative to have bonds of a common blood as well. Savarkar introduced the notion of 'race' to further consolidate his definition of Hindutva. The Hindus are 'not only a Nation but also a race—jati ... means a brotherhood, a race determined by a common origin—possessing a common blood'.[117] All Hindus had in their veins the blood of the Vedic fathers, the Sindhus.

The anulom and pratilom, literally, regular and inverse, marriage institutions had ensured the flow of common blood and had, indeed, given rise to a majority of castes in Hindusthan. Savarkar had to justify his thesis regarding common blood ties for his notion of Hindutva to be credible. He insisted that not only were intermarriages between the main four castes, and between the four castes in their pure form and the cross-born, i.e., those born out of such intermarriage between the castes, part of the eternal Hindu tradition, but intermarriages were even known between the tribals and the four castes. He proceeded to give a series of examples, a bulk of these from mythology.

The burden of providing evidence of common blood ties was an onerous one. Savarkar effortlessly moved from the realm of evidence to that of feeling. Nothing mattered but the heart and what it said:

> We *feel* that the same ancient blood that coursed through the veins of Ram and Krishna, Buddha and Mahavir, Nanak and Chaitanya, Basava and Madhava, of Rohildas and Tiruvelluvar courses throughout Hindudom from vein to vein, pulsates from heart to heart. We *feel* we are a JATI, a race bound together by the dearest ties of blood and therefore it must be so.[118]

To prevent commingling of blood, Savarkar persisted, was to build on sand. Especially when sexual attraction often proved to be a greater force than all the commands of all the prophets put together.

There was a moment in his narrative when Savarkar seemed to concede that the only legitimate claim that could be made was that the blood of mankind flowed in all people's veins.[119] But such concessions to the fundamental unity of mankind, he realized, did not make nations or further political agendas. Swiftly and emphatically, Savarkar returned to the theme of unity of all Hindus on the basis of blood ties. The most fundamental criterion that determined Hindutva, apart from a love of the land that stretched from Sindhu to Sindhu, was the inheritance of Hindu blood.[120]

Savarkar admitted that several Muslims might love Hindusthan as their fatherland. Those of them who were converts to Islam might even have Hindu blood in their veins. In Kashmir, there were Muslims who observed caste rules strictly. This was true of Christians in the south of India as well. Could these Muslims and Christians be called Hindus? Savarkar rejected their claim to Hindutva[121] because they lacked several other affirmations apart from sharing a common fatherland and blood ties.

The last and defining feature of Hindutva, therefore, was a commonly shared sanskriti, civilization. Hindus are one, says Savarkar, because they are a nation, a race and own a common sanskriti. The story of the civilization of a nation, he explains, is the story of its thoughts, its actions and its achievements.[122] Literature, art, history and social institutions are often the concrete manifestations of thought and action of a sanskriti. This is not to suggest that mutual differences among the Hindus do not exist. What they share in common is, however, greater than the sum total of their differences.

The common civilizational inheritance of the Hindus was further strengthened by the presence of Sanskrit as 'our mother tongue'.[123] Savarkar hastened to qualify this statement by saying that Sanskrit was the tongue of the mothers of the Hindu race. It was Sanskrit, he asserted, which formed the common link between all Indian languages. This common Hindu—the term here includes the Jains, Lingayats, Sikhs— inheritance extended to works of art and architecture. Hindus also shared principles of jurisprudence. Hindu law might betray some differences of detail but remains the basis for the unity of the race.

Common feasts and festivals and rites and rituals were the final arbiter of the essential unity of the Hindus. From a national and racial point of view, writes Savarkar, the different places of pilgrimage constituted the common inheritance of the Hindu race. The line of demarcation that divided Savarkar's categorization of Hindutva and the term 'Hinduism' that he was so much at pains to distance himself from was very thin:

> The Rathyatra festival at Jagannath, the Vaishakhi at Amritsar, the Kumbha and Ardhakumbha, all these great gatherings had been the real and living congress of our people that kept the current of life and the thought coursing throughout our body politic. The quaint customs and ceremonies and sacraments they involve, observed by some as a religious duty, by others

> as social amenities that he can live best only through the common and corporate life of the Hindu race.[124]

A Muslim, argued Savarkar, could never be part of Hindutva because he did not own up to and identify with the Hindu sanskriti as a whole. They belonged to an alien cultural matrix. Their heroes, their objects of worship and their fairs and festivals had little in common with the Hindus. It was imperative for a Hindu to have 'uncommon and loving attachment to his racial Sanskriti'.[125]

Could Bohras and Khojas be counted as Hindus?[126] Savarkar was willing to admit them though they might differ from Hindus regarding certain festivals or may add a few more heroes to the existing list. This was because they loved Hindusthan as their fatherland, possessed in most cases unadulterated Hindu blood. Further, they loved and worshipped the ten incarnations of Vishnu, only adding Prophet Muhammad as the eleventh. Their love of Hindu history and of Hindu heroes was unquestioned, and so was their fidelity to Hindu law. From the perspective of rashtra, jati and sanskriti, Bohras and Khojas identified with Hindutva and were undeniably Hindus.

Savarkar then went on to provide a comprehensive definition of Hindutva:

> We Hindus are not only a Rashtra, a Jati, but as a consequence of being both, own a common Sanskriti expressed, preserved chiefly and originally through Sanskrit, the real mother tongue of our race. Everyone who is a Hindu inherits this Sanskriti and owes his spiritual being to it as truly as he owes his physical one to the land and the blood of his forefathers.[127]

This explanation still leaves the question 'Who is a Hindu?' unanswered. Hinduism presupposed an independent conception of the Hindu, said Savarkar, which excluded several 'Hindu' communities from affirming allegiance to Hindutva. The question 'Who is a Hindu?' could not be answered by a handful of 'these gentlemen',[128] who arbitrarily go on to determine the essential tenets of Hinduism.

Uncomfortable with the reduction of Hinduism to a system of religion that the majority of the Hindu people follow, Savarkar sought to redefine Hinduism itself. He insisted that while the majority of Hindus might follow what they call orthodox Hinduism, heterodox communities were equally well within their rights to reject the authority of the dharmashastras.[129] All heterodox communities were Hindus despite their rejection of the customs and tenets of the orthodox, and hence majority, religion as a bunch of superstitions.

If Hinduism could not denote the inclusion of both the orthodox and the heterodox, Savarkar asserted, the term Hinduism ought to be dropped altogether. Unity was of the essence for a nation; unity of race and faith were paramount in the task of building a nation. To achieve the goals of political Hindutva, Savarkar made an audacious attempt to redefine Hinduism:

> The word Hindu has been derived from the word Sindhu, the Indus, meaning primarily all the people who reside in the land that extends from Sindhu to Sindhu, Hinduism must necessarily mean the religion or the religions that are peculiar and native to this land and these people.[130]

Hinduism could not, therefore, exclude religions that were 'native' to Hindusthan. What about the proliferation of systems of philosophy, customs and rituals?

> If we are unable to reduce the different tenets and beliefs to a single system of religion then the only way would be to cease to maintain that Hinduism is a system and to say that it is a set of systems consistent with, or if you like, contradictory or even conflicting with each other.[131]

The manner in which Hinduism was defined remained a peripheral concern with Savarkar. A protracted discussion on Hinduism would only open a can of worms in terms of doctrinal plurality and local variations in matters of faith. He was clear that no amount of definitional jugglery ought to impede the unity of the Hindu nation and the unity of faith and race:

> But in no case can you advance this failure to determine the meaning of Hinduism as a ground to doubt the existence of the Hindu nation itself or worse still to commit a sacrilege in hurting the feelings of our Avaidik brethren and Vaidik Hindu brethren alike, by relegating any of them to the non-Hindu pale.[132]

The religion of the majority Hindus could, therefore, be referred to as Sanatana dharma or *shruti-smriti-puranokta dharma,* while the 'remaining Hindus' could continue to call themselves by names such as Sikh dharma, Jain dharma, Buddha dharma or Arya dharma.[133] Only in the generic sense would the term 'Hindu dharma' or 'Hinduism' denote them.

Hinduism, therefore, was a word that ought to be applied to all the religious beliefs that the different communities of the Hindu people hold. This was Savarkar's categorical position before he defined Hindu dharma, a term or a category that was not to be conflated with Hinduism:

> This is Hindu Dharma—the conclusion of conclusions arrived at by harmonizing the detailed experience of all the schools of religious thought—Vaidik, Sanatani, Jain, Buddha, Sikha or Devasamaji. Each one and every one of those systems or sects which are the direct descendants and developments of the religious beliefs, Vaidik and non-Vaidik, that obtained in the land of the Sapta Sindhus or in the other unrecorded communities in other parts of India in the Vedic period, belong to and is an integral part of Hindu dharma.[134]

Hindu dharma included all sects and systems and Sindhusthan was the land of their revelation and birth.

Savarkar then returned to the question 'Who is a Hindu' and now offered a definition that has shaped and influenced political discourse to this day:

> We have found that the first important essential qualification of a Hindu is that to him the land that extends from Sindhu to Sindhu is the Fatherland (Pitribhu), the Motherland (Matribhu), the land of his patriarchs and forefathers ... [T]his land is the birth-place—the Matribhu (motherland) and the Pitribhu (fatherland)—of that Tatvajnana (philosophy) which in its religious aspect is signified as Hindu Dharma

> ... Hindu Dharma of all shades and schools, lives and grows and has its being in the atmosphere of Hindu culture, and the Dharma of a Hindu being so completely identified with the land of the Hindus, this land to him is not only Pitribhu but a Punyabhu, not only a fatherland but a holyland.[135]

Muslims and Christians have their lands of piety and pilgrimage beyond the territorial limits of Hindusthan. Their love and allegiance, therefore, were divided. They could never be participants in a common civilization or sanskriti, a prerequisite of Hindutva.

The future Indian polity needed a foundation. Savarkar was clear that this was to be provided by 'that portion of its citizens whose interests and history and aspirations are most closely bound up with the land and who thus provide the real foundation to the structure of their national state'.[136] This foundation and essence of national life was to be Hindutva:

> If you call it an Indian Nation it is merely an English synonym for the Hindu Nation. To us Hindus, Hindusthan and India mean one and the same thing. We are Indians because we are Hindus and vice versa.[137]

Muslims were condemned to be a minority community. In free India, Savarkar unambiguously stated, minorities will have rights according to the proportion of population and merit. 'India must be a Hindu land,' he says, 'reserved for the Hindus.'[138]

After resuming his public career in 1937, Savarkar had to contend with several contradictions in his own life and thought. As early as 1913, Savarkar had made his peace with British rule in India.[139] In a petition dated 14 November 1913, Savarkar wrote to the Home Member of the Government of India asking for clemency and assuring cooperation:

> In the end may I remind your honour to be so good as to go through the petition for clemency, that I had sent in 1911, and to sanction it for being forwarded to the Indian Government. The latest development of the Indian politics and the conciliating policy of the government have thrown open the constitutional line once more. Now no man having the good of India and Humanity at heart will blindly step on the thorny paths which in the excited and hopeless situation of India in 1906-1907 beguiled us from the path of peace and progress. Therefore if the government in their manifold beneficence and mercy release me, I for one cannot but be the staunchest advocate of constitutional progress and loyalty to the English government which is the foremost condition of that progress ... If we be released the people will instinctively raise a shout of joy and gratitude to the government, who knows how to forgive and correct, more than how to chastise and avenge ... I am ready to serve the government in any capacity they like, for as my conversion is conscientious so I hope my future conduct would be ... The Mighty alone can afford to be merciful and therefore where else can the prodigal son return but to the parental doors of the government?[140]

The 'black' sword lusting after 'white' blood in the essay on 1857 had converted. While he continued to demand full independence for India in his public pronouncements after 1937, his energies were directed more towards furthering arguments in favour of a Hindu Rashtra and splenetic outbursts against the Muslims.

Territorial nationalism was an issue that came in the way of Savarkar's vision of a Hindu Rashtra. Western education, Savarkar held, had deracinated Hindus and distanced them from their Hinduness. They took to territorial nationalism, which was premised on transcending religion, race and culture. Neither the Hindus nor the Muslims, he felt, would be able to abandon their religious identities and transform themselves into being patriots alone. Moreover, Muslims had little faith in territorial nationalism. Their sole aim was to convert all Hindus to Islam, bring about a pan-Islamic unity and dominate the Hindus. The Congress too had supported territorial nationalism, not realizing that 'in the formation of Nations, religious, racial, cultural and historical affinities count immensely more than their territorial unity'.[141] Territorial nationalism would only help the Muslim minority to convert Hindus, especially the lower castes, and increase their population with greater rapidity. Lack of recognition of Hindus as the 'original' and 'rightful' claimants to India would ultimately work in favour of the Muslims.

Independent India would be a state that would not recognize religion, caste, creed, sect or race. It will, asserts Savarkar, be founded on a 'one man, one vote' principle. This would automatically ensure that the Hindus, who formed a majority, would rule. Even the Muslims, despite their perfidy and fanaticism, would have rights. But they would never be loyal to India. Territorial nationalism was unknown to them. Here Savarkar cited the case of the Muslim League threatening to play the part of the Sudetan Germans if their demands were not met. Savarkar warned that if the Muslims were allowed to grow stronger, they could indeed play the part of the Sudetan Germans. But if Hindus grew stronger over a period of time—here Savarkar is at his diabolical 'best'—they would ensure that Muslims of the League type would have to 'play the part of German-Jews instead'.[142]

After 1937, Savarkar's pronouncements were littered with examples of dire warnings to the Muslims. Here are a few examples:

> When we will be in a position to retaliate thus in this wise and do retaliate, the Moslems will come to their senses in a day ... Knowing that every attempt to tyrannize the Hindus is sure to recoil on themselves and react for the worse on Moslem interests in all India—the Moslems will learn to behave as good boys.[143]

> On the whole the time has come when our Moslem countrymen should realize that even in their own interests they should accept the inevitable and should cease amusing themselves with airy nothings. They must count with realities, they must know they are in a minority and that there is not the slightest chance now left for them to reduce the present majority of the Hindus in any appreciable measure.[144]

In 1942, Savarkar was exhorting the Muslims to abandon their mad dreams of ruling India again. He was convinced that only through confrontation with the non-self, anti-Hindu forces as he terms them, could the resurrection, renaissance and rejuvenation of the Hindu nation become a reality. This was the lesson of history.

*

Savarkar lived for nineteen years in independent India. His ideal of Hindavi Swaraj remained a pipe dream in his lifetime. India did not become 'Turksthan' either. He continued to advocate his brand of Hindutva and wrote and spoke extensively on the security and defence of India. On 26 January 1950, the day India became a republic, Savarkar issued a statement[145] advocating a 'tit for tat' policy towards all real and potential enemies in order for India to survive and succeed. In 1961, he was arguing in favour of military strength as the only criterion for strength and greatness in the present-day world. He believed that a Hitler would be preferable to a democratic government that was weak and ineffective.

In his will, Savarkar decreed that his body be cremated in an electric crematorium without religious ceremonies. Only Vedic hymns could be chanted and no shraddha or pindadaan ceremonies ought to be performed after his death. Only mechanized transport ought to carry his body to the crematorium. In his life, Savarkar ate simple, was fond of fried fish, egg curry, relished ice cream and shrikhand, drank a glass of whisky in his old age, and was partial to chocolates, jintan and snuff.[146] He knew that he would either be seen by history as a daydreamer or as a prophet:

> If you wish, O Hindus, to prosper as a great and glorious Hindu Nation under the sun, and you well have a claim on it, that State must be established under the Hindu Flag. This dream would be realized during this or coming generation. If it is not realized, I may be styled a day-dreamer, but if it comes true, I would stand forth as its prophet.[147]

Savarkar was both a daydreamer and a prophet. He was an angry, resentful, vengeful, violent and intolerant prophet. The RSS, VHP, BJP and Bajrang Dal continue to further his legacy of Hindu jihad.

NOTES

1. Introduction

1. First published in December 2003 by Penguin/Viking. It was withdrawn from Penguin to protest against the publisher's decision to withdraw and pulp Wendy Doniger's book, *The Hindus, An Alternative History*.
2. Ronald Christ's interview with Jorge Luis Borges published in *Latin American Writers at Work*, edited by George Plimpton, The Modern Library, New York, 2003, p. 41.
3. *New York Review of Books*, 10 February 2011.
4. David N. Lorenzen, *Who Invented Hinduism? Essays on Religion in History*, Yoda Press, New Delhi, 2006.
5. Eiji Oguma, *A Genealogy of 'Japanese' Self-Images*, Trans Pacific Press, Melbourne, 2002.
6. I am deeply indebted to Professor Sasheej Hegde for a long note he wrote commenting on the themes in this book and on subsequent development of ideas around the theme of Hindu identity and the politics of Hindu nationalism.
7. I use the word 'theology' in absence of a better word to indicate an ongoing conversation about the central doctrines of a faith.

8. I have slightly paraphrased Edward Said's excellent articulation of this point. See Daniel Barenboim & Edward Said, *Parallels and Paradoxes: Explorations in Music and Society, Edited and with a preface by Ara Guzelimian*, Bloomsbury, London, 2003.
9. David Shulman, *Dark Hope: Working for Peace in Israel and Palestine,* Chicago University Press, Chicago, 2007.

2. Dayananda Saraswati

1. Swami Dayananda Saraswati, *Light of Truth,* Sarvadeshik Arya Pratinidhi Sabha, New Delhi, 2002 reprint, p. 2.
2. S.N. Mukherjee, *Sir William Jones: A Study in Eighteenth Century British Attitudes to India,* Sangam Books, London, 1987; Garland Cannon, 'The Indian Affair of Sir William Jones', in *Asian Affairs*, Vol. IX, Part III, October 1978.
3. Charles Grant, 'Observations', *Parliamentary Papers,* Vol. X, paper 282 (1812–1813), pp. 5–112.
4. *Satyarthaprakash*, p. 2.
5. Ibid., p. 3.
6. Ibid.
7. Ibid., p. 6.
8. Baruch Spinoza, *Early Philosophical Writings,* Bobbs-Merrill Company Inc., New York, p. 13.
9. *Satyarthaprakash*, pp. 6–9.
10. There is an elaborate discussion in *Satyarthaprakash* about the soul. At a later stage, this would be discussed briefly. For the present argument, it is sufficient to point out that Dayananda sees the soul as completely distinct from God.
11. *Satyarthaprakash*, p. 9.

12. Ibid., p. 204.
13. Ibid., p. 74.
14. Ibid.
15. Ibid.
16. Ibid., p. 75.
17. Ibid., p. 237.
18. Ibid., p. 219.
19. Ibid.
20. Ibid., p. 264.
21. Ibid., p. 266.
22. Ibid., pp. 316–17.
23. Ibid., pp. 330–34.
24. Ibid., p. 320.
25. Details of the chapter on Raja Dharma are incidental to the present argument. They will be referred to in the discussion on caste.
26. *Satyarthaprakash*, p. 267.
27. Ibid., pp. 469–70.
28. Ibid., p. 335.
29. Ibid., pp. 343–44.
30. Ibid., pp. 360–01.
31. Ibid.
32. Ibid., p. 363.
33. Ibid., p. 364.
34. Ibid., p. 365.
35. Ibid., p. 371.
36. Ibid., p. 372.
37. Ibid., p. 406.
38. Ibid., pp. 406–07.
39. Ibid., pp. 410–11.
40. Ibid., p. 414.
41. Ibid., p. 431.
42. Ibid., p. 442.
43. Ibid., p. 443.

44. Ibid., p. 526.
45. Ibid.
46. Ibid., p. 540.
47. Ibid.
48. Ibid., p. 549.
49. Ibid., p. 554.
50. Ibid., pp. 406–07.
51. Ibid., p. 591.
52. Ibid., p. 590.
53. Ibid., pp. 594–05.
54. Ibid.
55. Ibid., p. 612.
56. Ibid., p. 621.
57. Ibid., p. 619.
58. Ibid., p. 618.
59. Ibid., p. 628.
60. Ibid., p. 619.
61. Ibid., p. 652.
62. Ibid., p. 660.
63. Ibid., p. 664.
64. Ibid., p. 663.
65. Ibid., p. 667.
66. Ibid., p. 666.
67. *The Koran*, translated by N.J. Dawood, Penguin Books, 1990 impression, pp. 28–29.
68. *Satyarthaprakash*, p. 666.
69. Ibid., p. 677.
70. Ibid., p. 28.
71. Ibid., p. 40.
72. Ibid., p. 78.
73. Ibid., p. 79.
74. Ibid., p. 103.
75. Ibid., p. 167.
76. Ibid., p. 197.

77. Ibid., p. 382.
78. Ibid., p. 398.
79. Ibid., p. 475.
80. Sri Aurobindo, *Bankim, Tilak, Dayananda*, Sri Aurobindo Ashram, Pondicherry, 1940, p. 34.
81. Ibid.
82. Swami Vivekananda, *The Complete Works of Swami Vivekananda*, Volume V, Advaita Ashrama, 1936, p. 99.

3. Sri Aurobindo

1. Sri Aurobindo, *On Himself*, Sri Aurobindo Ashram, Pondicherry, 1985 impression, p. 34.
2. Sri Aurobindo, *Karmayogin, Early Political Writings—2*, Sri Aurobindo Birth Centenary Library, Pondicherry, 1972, p. 10.
3. Sri Aurobindo, *India's Rebirth*, Paris and Mysore, Institut De Recherches Evolutives and Mira Aditi, 2000 edition, pp. 120–21.
4. Sri Aurobindo, *On Nationalism*, Sri Aurobindo Ashram, Poundicherry, 1996 edition.
5. Sri Aurobindo, 'New Lamps for the Old—II,' in *On Nationalism*, p. 17.
6. Sri Aurobindo, *Bande Mataram*, Pondicherry, Sri Aurobindo Ashram, 1973 edition, pp. 235–6.
7. *On Nationalism*, pp. 335–59.
8. Ibid., p. 337.
9. *India's Rebirth*, p. 123.
10. Ibid., p. 144.
11. *Bande Mataram*, p. 122.
12. Sri Aurobindo, *Essays on the Gita*, First and Second Series, 2 volumes, Arya Publishing House, Calcutta, 1937 and 1942.

13. *Essays on the Gita,* First Series, p. 66.
14. Ibid., pp. 74–5.
15. Ibid., pp. 93–95.
16. Ibid., pp. 273–4.
17. Ibid., p. 83.
18. *Essays on the Gita*, Second Series, p. 275.
19. Ibid., pp. 277–78.
20. Ibid., p. 281.
21. Ashis Nandy, *The Intimate Enemy*, Oxford University Press, Delhi, 1983, p. 78.
22. Ananda K. Coomaraswamy, *Spiritual Authority and Temporal Power in the Indian Theory of Government*, IGNCA and Oxford University Press, 1993, pp. 1–2.
23. *On Nationalism,* p. 386. Here 'Aryan thought' stands for an uncorrupted, pure and unsullied version of Hindu thought, which had recourse to first principles as put forth in the Vedas and the Upanishads.
24. Ibid., p. 467.
25. *India's Rebirth*, p. 106.
26. *On Nationalism*, p. 55.
27. Ibid., pp. 66–67.
28. Ibid., p. 67.
29. Ibid., p. 72.
30. *Bande Mataram*, p. 468.
31. *On Nationalism*, p. 351.
32. Ibid.
33. Ibid., p. 349.
34. Sri Aurobindo, *Bankim-Tilak-Dayananda,* Sri Aurobindo Ashram, Pondicherry, 1970, p. 7.
35. Ibid., pp. 10–11.
36. *Bande Mataram.*, pp. 234–35.
37. *On Nationalism*, p. 328.
38. Ibid., p. 383.

39. *India's Rebirth*, p. 93.
40. *On Nationalism*, p. 179.
41. *The Human Cycle*, pp. 166–67.
42. *India's Rebirth*, p. 139.
43. Ibid., p. 82.
44. *On Nationalism*, p. 179.
45. Ibid., p. 228.
46. Ibid., p. 375.
47. Ibid., p. 385.
48. *India's Rebirth*, p. 143.
49. Ibid., p. 143.
50. *On Nationalism*, p. 403.
51. Ibid., p. 389.
52. Ibid., p. 390.
53. Ibid.
54. Ibid., p. 481.
55. Ibid., p. 483.
56. Ibid.
57. Ibid.
58. Ibid., p. 484.
59. Ibid.
60. *On Nationalism*, pp. 484–85.
61. *India's Rebirth*, p. 164.
62. *On Nationalism*, p. 483.
63. *India's Rebirth*, p. 165.
64. Ibid.
65. Ibid., p. 166.
66. Ibid., p. 167.
67. Ibid., p. 177.
68. Ibid., pp. 220–1.
69. Ibid.

4. Swami Vivekananda

1. See A.B. Vajpayee's musings from Goa, 31 December 2002, PTI text.
2. *The Complete Works of Swami Vivekananda* (henceforth, *CW*), Vol. VIII, Advaita Ashrama, Calcutta, 1999 impression (first published in 1951), p. 163.
3. *CW*, Vol. VIII, p. 174. I have chosen to translate 'naradeva deva' differently from the given definition, which is 'Lord of Men'. This is too literal a translation and does not convey the Vedantic sense in which I believe Vivekananda would have coined it.
4. *CW*, Vol. VII, Advaita Ashrama, Almora, 1927, second edition, pp. 83–84.
5. *CW*, Vol. VII, p. 22.
6. Ibid., p. 22.
7. Ibid., p. 90.
8. Ibid., p. 138.
9. Ibid., pp. 204–05.
10. *CW*, Vol. VI, Advaita Ashrama, Almora, 1926, p. 380.
11. *CW*, Vol. VII, p. 400.
12. *CW*, Vol. VIII, pp. 263–64.
13. Ibid., p. 263.
14. Ibid., p. 264.
15. Ibid., p. 522–3.
16. *CW*, Vol. VII, pp. 83–84.
17. *CW*, Vol. I, Advaita Ashrama, Calcutta, 2000, twenty-third impression, pp. 3–4.
18. Ibid., p. 3.
19. *CW*, Vol. I, pp. 6–20.
20. Ibid., p. 13
21. Ibid.
22. Ibid., p. 17.

23. Ibid.
24. Ibid., p. 393.
25. Ibid., p. 348.
26. *CW*, Vol. III, Advaita Ashrama, Almora, 1932, p. 113.
27. *CW*, Vol. IV, Advaita Ashrama, Almora, 1932, p. 175.
28. *CW*, Vol. I, p. 376.
29. Ibid., pp. 379–80.
30. *CW*, Vol. III, p. 249.
31. *CW*, Vol. I, p. 117.
32. Ibid., p. 184.
33. Ibid.
34. *CW*, Vol. IV, p. 256.
35. *CW*, Vol. VIII, pp. 202–03.
36. *CW*, Vol. I, pp. 481–04.
37. Ibid., p. 481. It is tempting to see the influence of Thomas Carlyle's essay on the Prophet, published in 1841, on Vivekananda. See, 'The Hero As Prophet. Mahomet: Islam', in Thomas Carlyle, *Heroes and Hero-Worship*, Chapman and Hall Limited, 1907 edition.
38. Ibid., p. 482.
39. *CW*, Vol. I, p. 482.
40. *CW*, Vol. II, p. 333.
41. Ibid., p. 368.
42. Ibid., pp. 350–51.
43. Ibid.
44. *CW*, Vol. IV, p. 122. He usually means the Sufis. Vivekananda felt that Sufism had been influenced by Vedanta and had attained the touch of the Divine.
45. Ibid., p. 122.
46. *CW*, Vol. III, pp. 369-70.
47. *CW*, Vol. IV, p. 379.
48. Ibid., p. 318.
49. Ibid., pp. 136–37.

50. *CW*, Vol. II, p. 351.
51. Ibid.
52. Ibid.
53. *CW*, Vol. IV, p. 143.
54. *CW*, Vol. II, p. 24.
55. Ibid., p. 106.
56. *CW*, Vol. I, pp. 331–32.
57. Ibid., p. 329.
58. *CW*, Vol. II, p. 372.
59. Ibid.
60. *CW*, Vol. VI, pp. 103–04.
61. *CW*, Vol. I, p. 341.
62. Ibid., p. 388.
63. Ibid., pp. 384-85.
64. Ibid.
65. *CW*, Vol. I, p. 385. The emphasis in the quote is mine. Also see Vivekananda's extremely poetic formulation of the same idea in Vol. III, p. 115.
66. *CW*, Vol. IV, p. 289. Emphasis mine.
67. *CW*, Vol. III, pp. 187–88.
68. Ibid., p. 132.
69. *CW*, Vol. IV, pp. 150–83.
70. Ibid., pp. 169–70.
71. *CW*, Vol. III, p. 105.
72. Ibid.
73. Ibid.
74. Ibid., p. 292.
75. *CW*, Vol. IV, p. 255.
76. Ibid., pp. 245–47.
77. Ibid., p. 242.
78. Ibid., p. 243.
79. *CW*, Vol. III, p. 167.
80. *CW*, Vol. IV, p. 245.
81. Ibid., p. 245.

82. Ibid., p. 317.
83. Ibid.
84. *CW*, Vol. V, p. 19.
85. Ibid., p. 322.
86. *CW*, Vol. III, p. 293.
87. Ibid., p. 298.
88. *CW*, Vol. VI, pp. 224–5.
89. *CW*, Vol. VIII, p. 290.
90. *CW*, Vol. VI, p. 124.
91. *CW*, Vol. III, p. 290.
92. Ibid., p. 291.
93. *CW*, Vol. IV, p. 247.
94. *CW*, Vol. V, p. 240.
95. *CW*, Vol. VI, p. 343.
96. Ibid.
97. *CW*, Vol. IV, p. 270.
98. Ibid., p. 422.
99. Ibid., p. 423.
100. Ibid.
101. Ibid.
102. Ibid., p. 422.
103. *CW*, Vol. III, p. 270; also, *CW*, Vol. IV, pp. 424–5.
104. *CW*, Vol. IV, p. 313.
105. Ibid.
106. *CW*, Vol. V, p. 5, 11.
107. Ibid., p. 12.
108. *CW*, Vol. IV, pp. 421–22.
109. Ibid., p. 310.
110. *CW*, Vol. V, p. 40.
111. Ibid., pp. 374–77.
112. *CW*, Vol. VI, pp. 225–26.
113. *CW*, Vol. III, p. 242.
114. Ibid.
115. *CW*, Vol. V, p. 68.

116. Ibid., pp. 260–61.
117. Ibid., p. 304.
118. Ibid.
119. *CW*, Vol. VII, p. 417. Vivekananda is less emphatic on this aspect than Bankim before him, and Aurobindo who was his contemporary. While he spoke of Shakti worship, I maintain that it was not central to his scheme of regenerating India. There are instances of Vivekananda speaking of the mission of the Mother, but this allusion to Mother as Shakti remained peripheral at best. Some reasons for this have been suggested in Section I and Section V of this chapter.
120. See chapter on Sri Aurobindo.
121. *CW*, Vol. V, p. 87.
122. *CW*, Vol. IV, p. 337.
123. *CW*, Vol. V, p. 351.
124. *CW*, Vol. VIII, p. 481.
125. Ibid., pp. 355–56.
126. Ibid., p. 357.
127. *CW*, Vol. VI, p. 75.
128. Ibid., p. 87.
129. *CW*, Vol. VIII, p. 227.
130. Ibid., p. 263.
131. *CW*, Vol. III, p. 369.
132. Ibid., pp. 369-70.
133. Ibid., p. 220.
134. *CW*, Vol. III, p. 289.
135. Ibid., pp. 370–71.
136. Ibid. The allusion to the 'jewel' and the 'bird' is from popular stories. As long as the snake had a jewel on its head, it was indestructible. Similarly, giants and ogres had their souls interred in birds. They could not be killed as long as the bird lived. See *CW*, Vol. III, p. 369.

137. *CW*, Vol. V, pp. 361–62.
138. Ibid.
139. *CW*, Vol. III, p. 118. It would be safe to speculate that Savarkar may have been influenced by this argument as well as the etymological derivation of 'Hindu' from 'Sindhu'. Also see, *CW*, Vol. III, p. 228.
140. Ibid., p. 118.
141. Formally defined, dualism is any view that suggests two kinds of things in some domain as contrasted with a view according to which there is only one kind of thing in a domain. Vivekananda contrasts dualism with his brand of monism in the form of Advaita Vedanta.
142. *CW*, Vol. II, p. 141.
143. Ibid., p. 199.
144. Ibid., p. 201.
145. Ibid., pp. 240–41.
146. *CW*, Vol. II, p. 240.
147. *CW*, Vol. VIII, p. 308.
148. *CW*, Vol. V, p. 13.
149. *CW*, Vol. VI, pp. 354–55.
150. *CW*, Vol. III, p. 228.
151. *CW*, Vol. V, p. 289.
152. Ibid.
153. *CW*, Vol. III, p. 228.
154. Ibid., pp. 228–29.
155. Ibid., p. 229.
156. Ibid., p. 231.
157. Ibid., p. 332.
158. Ibid., pp. 332–33.
159. Ibid., p. 333.
160. Ibid., p. 152.
161. Ibid., pp. 333–34.
162. *CW*, Vol. V, p. 64.

163. Ibid. The yoga-perception form means the ritualistic practice of Buddhism.
164. *CW*, Vol. III, p. 230.
165. *CW*, Vol. II, p. 247.
166. *CW*, Vol. III, p. 347.
167. *CW*, Vol. VIII, pp. 124–25.
168. *CW*, Vol. II, pp. 84–85.
169. *CW*, Vol. VII, p. 161.
170. Ibid., p. 175.
171. *CW*, Vol. VII, p. 220.
172. *CW*, Vol. VIII, p. 100.
173. Ibid., pp. 306–07.
174. *CW*, Vol. VII, p. 341.
175. *CW*, Vol. VIII, p. 76.
176. *CW*, Vol. VII, p. 341.
177. *CW*, Vol. VIII, p. 76.
178. *CW*, Vol. VII, p. 181.
179. *CW*, Vol. V, p. 39.
180. Ibid., p. 96.
181. *CW*, Vol. VIII, p. 299.
182. *CW*, Vol. VI, pp. 375–76.
183. Ibid., p. 376.
184. *CW*, Vol. VIII, pp. 79–80.
185. *CW*, Vol. VI, pp. 302–03.
186. *CW*, Vol. Ill, p. 72.
187. *CW*, Vol. VII, p. 435. See details in Part III of this chapter.
188. *CW*, Vol. I, p. 21.
189. Ibid., p. 23.
190. Ibid. pp. 348–49.
191. *CW*, Vol. III, p. 230.
192. *CW*, Vol. IV, p. 131.
193. Ibid.

194. Ibid., p. 132.
195. *CW*, Vol. III, p. 264.
196. *CW*, Vol. IV, p. 272.
197. Ibid., p. 273.
198. *CW*, Vol. V, pp. 317–18.
199. *CW*, Vol. III, pp. 264–65. The reference to degraded Buddhism is to the introduction of tantric elements in Buddhism after the death of the Buddha as well as the introduction of women in viharas.
200. *CW*, Vol. VI, p. 86.
201. *CW*, Vol. V, pp. 206–07.
202. *CW*, Vol. VI, p. 86.
203. Ibid., p. 132.
204. Ibid., pp. 194–05.
205. *CW*, Vol. VII, pp. 38–39. 'Sankara's intellect was sharp like the razor; —he was a good argumentator and a scholar, no doubt of that, but he had no great liberality; his heart too seems to have been like that. Besides, he used to take great pride in his Brahminism...' Vol. VII, p. 115.
206. Ibid., pp. 38–39.
207. Ibid., p. 57.
208. Ibid., pp. 116–17.
209. *CW*, Vol. VIII, pp. 92–105.
210. Ibid., pp. 96–97.
211. Ibid., p. 99.
212. Ibid.
213. Ibid., pp. 100–101.
214. Ibid., p. 101.
215. Ibid.
216. *CW*, Vol. VII, pp. 128–29.
217. Ibid., p. 21.

5. Vinayak Damodar Savarkar

1. Dhananjay Keer, *Veer Savarkar*, Popular Prakashan, Bombay, 1988 (Third Edition), p. 4.
2. Vinayak Damodar Savarkar, *Savarkar Samagra*, Volume 1, Prabhat Prakashan, Delhi, 2000–03, pp. 152–53.
3. Ibid., p. 152.
4. V.D. Savarkar, *Hindutva*, Swatantryaveer Savarkar Rashtriya Smarak, Mumbai, 1999 (Seventh Edition), pp. 9–10.
5. Ibid.
6. See *Hindutva*, p. 26; also, 'How Hindus Ought to Write and Read the History of their Nation', *Savarkar Samagra*, Volume 5, pp. 443–44.
7. *Hindutva*, p. 26.
8. Ibid., p. 28.
9. Ibid., p. 28.
10. V.B. Savarkar, *Hindu-Pad-Padashahi*, Bharati Sahitya Sadan, New Delhi, 1971 (Fourth Edition), first published in 1925, p. 20.
11. Ibid. p. 196.
12. Ibid., pp. 196–97.
13. Ibid., pp. 197–98.
14. Ibid.
15. Ibid., pp. 21–22.
16. Ibid.
17. 'The War of Independence of 1857', *Savarkar Samagra*, Volume 5, p. 106.
18. Ibid.
19. Ibid., pp. 232–33.
20. Ibid.
21. 'The Rise, Fall and Destruction of Muslim Theocracy', in *Savarkar Samagra*, Volume 5, pp. 506–32.

22. Ibid., p. 507.
23. Ibid.
24. Ibid., p. 512.
25. Ibid., p. 513.
26. Ibid.
27. 'Uprooting of Arab Culture from Turkey by Kemal Pasha', in *Savarkar Samagra,* Volume 5, pp. 518–32.
28. Ibid., p. 519.
29. Ibid.
30. Ibid., pp. 519–20.
31. Ibid., p. 520.
32. 'Sangeet Uhshraap', in *Savarkar Samagra,* Volume 4, pp. 19–146. (author's translation).
33. Ibid., pp. 122–23.
34. Ibid., p. 123.
35. Ibid., p. 124.
36. *Savarkar Samagra*, Volume 3.
37. Ibid.
38. *Hindutva*, pp. 31–44.
39. *Hindu-Pad-Padashahi*, p. 28.
40. Ibid., p. 234.
41. Ibid., pp. 234–5.
42. 'Presidential Address—19th Session of the Akhil Bharatiya Hindu Mahasabha, Karnavati (Ahmedabad), 1937', in *Hindu Rashtra Darshan,* pp. 14–15.
43. Ibid., p. 20.
44. Ibid., p. 24.
45. Ibid., p. 49.
46. 'The War of Independence of 1857', in *Savarkar Samagra,* Volume 5, pp. 19–440.
47. Ibid., p. 19.
48. Ibid., p. 27.
49. Ibid.
50. Ibid., pp. 30–31.

51. Ibid., p. 60.
52. Giuseppe Mazzini, *On Nationality*, p. 226.
53. *1857,* p. 24.
54. Ibid., p. 72.
55. Ibid., p. 106.
56. Ibid.
57. Ibid., pp. 96–97.
58. Ibid., pp. 100–04.
59. Ibid., p. 164.
60. Ibid., p. 196.
61. Ibid., p. 256.
62. Ibid., p. 257.
63. Ibid., p. 202.
64. Ibid., p. 229.
65. Ibid., pp. 228–29.
66. Ibid.
67. Ibid.
68. Ibid., p. 230.
69. *Hindu Rashtra Darshan*, p. 154.
70. Ibid., p. 149.
71. Ibid., p. 154.
72. *Hindutva,* p. 12.
73. Ibid., pp. 12–13.
74. Ibid., p. 13.
75. Ibid., p. 13.
76. Ibid., p. 13.
77. Ibid., p. 13.
78. Ibid., p. 14.
79. Ibid., p. 15.
80. *Savarkar Samagra,* Volume 4, pp. 149–187.
81. *Sanyastha Khadga*, p. 226.
82. Ibid. pp. 255–80.
83. See Lewis Namier's fine essay, 'Nationality and Liberty', in *Vanished Supremacies,* Penguin Books, London, 1962, pp. 55–60.

84. Also see Denis Mack Smith's definitive biography of Mazzini for the distinction Mazzini made between nationality and nationalism. Denis Mack Smith, *Mazzini,* Yale University Press, New Haven and London, 1994, pp. 12–13, pp. 154–59.
85. Giuseppe Mazzini, 'Europe: Its Condition and Prospects', *Essays: Selected from the Writings, Literary, Political and Religious of Joseph Mazzini,* William Clark (ed.), Walter Scott, London, 1880, p. 266.
86. Denis Mack Smith, *Mazzini*, p. 218.
87. Ibid., p. 114.
88. *1857*, p. 20.
89. *Hindu-Pad-Padashahi*, p. 216.
90. *Savarkar Samagra,* Volume 1, pp. 446–70.
91. Ibid., p. 463.
92. *Hindu Rashtra Darshan*, 1937 address, p. 22.
93. Ibid., p. 5.
94. Ibid., p. 14.
95. Ibid., p. 16.
96. Ibid., p. 22.
97. Ibid., p. 16; also, pp. 14, and 27.
98. Ibid., p. 10.
99. *Hum kaun hain? Apne ko pehechaaney*, Hindu Mahasabha, New Delhi, 1961, p. 3.
100. *Hindutva*, p. 1.
101. Ibid., p. 2.
102. Ibid., p. 50.
103. Ibid.
104. Ibid., p. 3.
105. Ibid., p. 6.
106. Ibid., p. 5.
107. Ibid., p. 7.
108. Ibid., pp. 7–8.
109. Ibid., p. 19.

110. Ibid., p. 20.
111. Ibid.
112. Ibid.
113. Ibid., p. 24.
114. Ibid., p. 28.
115. Ibid., p. 5l.
116. Ibid., p. 52.
117. Ibid., p. 53.
118. Ibid., p. 56. The emphasis on 'feel' in the quote is original to Savarkar.
119. Ibid.
120. Ibid., pp. 56–57.
121. Ibid., p. 57.
122. Ibid., p. 58.
123. Ibid., pp. 59–60.
124. Ibid., p. 62.
125. Ibid., p. 63.
126. Ibid.
127. Ibid., p. 62.
128. Ibid., p. 64.
129. Ibid., p. 66.
130. Ibid., p. 65.
131. Ibid., p. 65.
132. Ibid., p. 65.
133. Ibid., p. 67.
134. Ibid., p. 68.
135. Ibid., pp. 68–69.
136. Ibid., p. 87.
137. *Hindu Rashtra Darshan,* 1938 speech to the Hindu Mahasabha in Nagpur, p. 52.
138. Ibid., pp. 55–57.
139. See Suresh Sharma's thoughtful essay on Savarkar titled 'Savarkar's Quest for a Modern Hindu Consolidation', *Studies in Humanities and Social*

Sciences, Vol. II, No. 2, 1996, pp. 189–215, Shimla.

140. Petition from V.D. Savarkar (Convict No. 32778) to the Home Member of the Government of India, dated 14 November 1913, published in *Penal Settlement in Andamans,* edited by R.C. Majumdar, published by the Gazetteers Unit of the Union Ministry of Education.
141. *Hindu Rashtra Darshan*, pp. 47–8.
142. Ibid., p. 53.
143. Ibid., pp. 64–65.
144. Ibid., pp. 181–82.
145. *Thus Spake the Prophet,* Swatantryaveer Savarkar Rashtriya Smarak, Mumbai, 1998 imprint, p. 2.
146. Dhananjay Keer, Veer Savarkar, p. 476.
147. Ibid., p. 556.

INDEX

ACKNOWLEDGEMENTS

This book owes its new life to V.K. Karthika. She enthusiastically agreed to publish this volume after I withdrew its publication from the publishers who had originally published it in 2003. In a sense, Karthika was always associated with the book: she had signed the offer letter in 2002 when the book was first commissioned. The book, Karthika and the author in this sense share a past that is behind us. My deep and sincere gratitude to her for believing in the book and giving it a new lease of life.

Shantanu Ray Chaudhuri continues to be a boon editor. He has, yet again, saved me from errors that have escaped my eyes. I thank him for his meticulous attention to detail and all his help in the making of this volume. I thank Saurabh Garge for the cover of the book.

A NOTE ON TRANSLATIONS

All direct quotations cited in the book from *Savarkar Samagra* have been translated from Hindi and Marathi by the author. Substantial quotes have been indented and shown in the chapter on Savarkar. Other references from *Savarkar Samagra* are summaries of Savarkar's arguments that incorporate key phrases from the original along with reference to the original source. I have used the already existing translations in English of *Hindutva* and *Hindu-Pad-Padashahi* in the chapter. Citations from these two texts are not my translation.